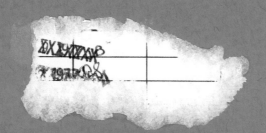

NEVADA

NEVADA

Land Of Discovery

David Beatty

Robert O. Beatty

FIB FIRST NATIONAL BANK OF NEVADA   1976

Contents

Standard Book Number: 0-9600972-1-X
Library of Congress Catalog Card Number: 76-4140
First National Bank of Nevada, Reno 89501
Licensee: R. O. Beatty & Associates, Boise 83702
Copyright © 1976, by First National Bank of Nevada
All rights reserved.
Printed in the United States of America

A Beatty Book

Foreword

I'm not sure that anything I can say about this book will do it justice. I could say that it's beautiful—but that's obvious. I could say that it tells the story of Nevada; that the photographers who contributed to it are some of the best in the country; or that it's fine reading from start to finish—and of course that would all be true.

But what I really want to say about this book is that it *is* Nevada, the whole picture—the heart, the spirit, the character, the indefinable something that makes this state unique.

First National Bank has been a part of life in Nevada since 1902. As our contribution to the nation's bicentennial, we are proud to have made this book possible.

A. M. Smith
Chairman of the Board and
Chief Executive Officer

Introduction

It's been fun putting this book together. We came into Nevada not really knowing what to expect, and trying not to predict what we'd find. Instead we gave serendipity free rein and let our experience of Nevada shape what went into the book. The variety of perception and the depth of feeling we soon discovered assured an authentic portrait.

We spent a lot of our time traveling the backroads—and certainly there's no better way to find out what Nevada really is. The immense expanse is simply overwhelming. It can be a little frightening sometimes, but it is also exhilarating. Life against such a backdrop takes on a richness and intensity not found elsewhere. Wherever we went, we found an unassuming directness in the people who have been attracted to this land and the independence it fosters—not only in Las Vegas and Reno, but also among the ranchers, farmers, and miners throughout the rest of Nevada.

The book is a blending of impressions, our own as well as those of many Nevadans, past and present. We haven't attempted a complete description of the obvious; rather, we have chosen to try to convey the beauty, the feeling, and the flavor of Nevada. Indeed, life does taste different in Nevada, and to appreciate that is what this book is all about.

David Beatty

Bob Beatty

Austin, Nevada
May, 1976

Coming to Grips with the Land

Nevada was a tough land to come to grips with. The vast geography of the Great Basin held out no invitation to the earliest explorers and settlers. They were confronted by a barren wilderness — sun-baked deserts, vanishing rivers, an arid desolation. No wonder this was the last part of the United States to be penetrated and explored by the white man.

The Spanish, who were the first to claim jurisdiction over the area, skirted this harsh, forbidding region in their exploration of North America. They were content to leave this section of their domain uncharted, calling the blank space left on their maps the "Northern Mystery." And wise they seemed, for a later explorer, having crossed Nevada, gave this description: "There is space and no atmosphere, soil and no verdure, mountains and no inspiration; the sky has no fleck in its glassy blue, the crusted land crumbles to dust under the feet, and nourishes no heartier growth than the sickly artemisia; the mountains are hot and bare. What blight, or drought or unfinished process of nature has left such a blot as this on the earth? It hardly seems to be earth at all."

Many have described the Nevada landscape in such terms, as if it were still in the throes of creation; yet it is this very character that gives the land its grandeur, its awesomeness. One cannot be touched by the first rays and shadows of a sunrise out in the reaches of Nevada without sensing upon the land a primordial wildness that will endure in spite of all the comings and goings and changings of man. I find this enriching, even inspiring.

The area wasn't always so formidable. At one time it was forested lakeland, supporting as rich and varied a flora and fauna as anywhere on the continent. Later, mountains were formed to the west, blocking the moist winds from the ocean. The Great Basin became a grassland, rangeland for the forebears of today's horses, camels, and antelope. Then about thirty million years ago Nevada was convulsed by volcanic activity. The crust of the earth broke open; lava and volcanic ash covered the land. The fractured, faulting earth lifted its edges to form the Sierra Nevada, the Pacific Coast Range, and the Wasatch, as well as the more than three hundred mountain ranges that make Nevada the most mountainous state in the Union.

At the onset of the Ice Age the climate turned wet again. Rains and glaciers fed rivers that could no longer find outlet to the sea. Scores of lakes began to form in the basins between the mountains, ultimately creating the mammoth Lake Lahontan—named for Baron Louis Armand de Lahontan, an early French explorer—which sprawled across eight thousand square miles of northwestern Nevada.

The ancient shoreline of that enormous body of water can still be seen, from as far south as Hawthorne to the Nevada-Oregon line, and from Winnemucca to the California border. Today, all that remains of Lahontan are two puddles, Pyramid and Walker lakes. For, as the glaciers receded and the climate warmed again, evaporation began to take its toll. The Sierra effectively blocked moisture from the Pacific, and the small

Desert homestead, Marietta

Resting wagon wheels, Denio

Petroglyphs, Big Horn Springs

Shoshone family

snow-fed streams could no longer keep pace with the desiccation caused by dry air and a relentlessly hot sun. This dehydration gave the land the arid, stark character it retains to this day. (The evaporation rate in some parts of Nevada equals seven feet of water a year.) Without moisture, no humus or soil could develop; without fertile soil, there could be no luxuriant vegetation or multitudes of wildlife.

The white man was by no means the first to inhabit the region. Long before he started his tentative explorations, Nevada was home to groups of Indians who sustained themselves in harmony with the uniquely demanding environment. Life was reduced to the basic necessity of gathering food, and in this these people were thoroughly ingenious. Roaming about the desert in small bands, they harvested almost anything of an edible nature. Nearly forty varieties of seeds were gathered; wild celery, sweet sage, and the blazing star were eaten, as were the roots and bulbs of the sego lily, camas, and wild caraway. Pine nuts were gathered in the fall. Insects such as crickets and locusts, and their larvae, were relished. The people of this desert culture were also hunters, mostly of lizards and rabbits, but also of the deer, antelope, and bighorn sheep that inhabited parts of the Great Basin. Fish from the lakes were another source of food. From the earliest times, baskets were used for gathering and storing the fruits of the land. The Washoe Indians later made basket-weaving an art form.

Southern Paiute hunter

Washoe basketry

Paiute basket weaver

In one sense, it was a groveling, tedious existence. White men called these Indians "Diggers" and classed them among the lowest, most miserable forms of humanity. But one explorer observed among them "a degree of happiness ... which civilized men, wearied with care and anxious pursuit, perhaps seldom enjoy." Primitive tribes, living on the edge of survival, always seem to enjoy a pleasant companionship among themselves, oblivious to what the future may hold.

Certainly, the desert Indians were unaware of the value another civilization was placing on a lowly rodent. Beaver felt hats were the fashion in Europe, and castor, a secretion of the beaver's musk glands, was thought to be a cure-all. Jedediah Smith, searching for new trapping grounds, traveled through southern Nevada along the Virgin and Colorado rivers in the fall of 1826, and back across central Nevada the following spring. He hoped to find the legendary San Buenaventura River, supposedly the Great Basin's outlet to the sea, and must have been disappointed when he found no river and no beaver. Peter Skene Ogden had more success. He entered Nevada from the north and found beaver along what he called the Unknown River, today known as the Humboldt.

As beaver became scarce elsewhere, other trapping parties crossed through Nevada; but it was John C. Frémont, "the Pathfinder," who first set out to actually explore and map the region. On January 10, 1844, after crossing a seemingly endless stretch of mountain and desert, Frémont's party looked

Sego lily

down upon "a sheet of green water [that] broke upon our eyes like the ocean.... For a long time we sat enjoying the view, for we had become fatigued with mountains, and the free expanse of moving waves was very grateful." Frémont's attention was attracted to an island whose outline reminded him of the pyramid of Cheops, suggesting a name for the lake.

In the spring the party crossed southern Nevada along the Spanish Trail, a trade route used by Mexican caravans between Santa Fe and California. The springs and meadows named Las Vegas by the Spanish provided welcome relief from the furnace-like heat and glare of this forsaken country. "Two narrow streams of clear water, four to five feet deep, gush suddenly, with a quick current, from two singularly large springs," Frémont noted. "...The taste of the water is good, but rather too warm to be agreeable; the temperature being 71 degrees in the one and 73 degrees in the other. They, however, afforded a delightful bathing place." As he continued across the desert, Frémont observed a peculiarity: "Throughout this nakedness of sand and gravel, were many beautiful plants and flowering shrubs, which occurred in many new species, and with greater variety than we had been accustomed to see in the most luxuriant prairie country."

The reports that Frémont and others sent east spurred many to seek opportunity in the West. The Humboldt River became a lifeline for those early California emigrants. But with the discovery of gold in 1849, the exodus overtaxed the land. Game and forage along the Humboldt were soon exhausted, prompting one pioneer to rename the river the Humbug—a mild epithet indeed, considering the hardship

Tortured land near Lake Mohave

Joshua trees and yucca, below Spring Mountains

John C. Frémont

Humboldt River beaver

Frémont's pyramid, Pyramid Lake

Genoa, 1863

Humboldt River

Registration Rock, High Rock Canyon

and misery that took place along its course. After crossing half a continent, thousands of weary pioneers had little to fall back on but their courage and determination, and many found that wasn't enough in the choking alkali and sand of the dreaded Forty Mile Desert. Life itself was abandoned in despair, as were the wagons, animals, and treasured possessions that had come so far. Only the hardy survived to drink at the Carson River and make their way over the Sierra.

Some found opportunity east of the Sierra, most notably John Reese, who in 1851 brought supplies from Salt Lake City to set up a permanent trading post, Mormon Station, later called Genoa. Other settlers followed, finding good pasture and farmland in the surrounding valleys. From Salt Lake City, Brigham Young was sending his followers out to colonize the expanding state of Deseret. They were sent to Las Vegas to secure a "Mormon Corridor" from Salt Lake City to southern California, and to the Carson Valley, where they established a thriving community.

The settlers found a good thing here. It was a demanding life, to be sure, but a vigorous, independent life as well, to match the self-reliance and fortitude they showed crossing the country. Descendents of those first Nevadans still reflect a durable vitality that we are hard put to find in the commotion of 20th Century America. Ione Hawkins Fettic has lived most of her eighty-nine years in Genoa, and to talk with her is to be inspired. There's a liveliness and zest in her manner that can come only from living a full, free life.

John Mackay

Comstock miner

Placer mining, Gold Canyon

The presence of gold in Nevada was casually noted by William Prouse in 1850. Following his discovery, a small mining colony grew up in Gold Canyon. The miners were often hampered by a lack of water to run their sluices, and by a heavy "blue muck" that clogged the placer operations. It wasn't until 1859, when the ledge later known as the Comstock Lode was discovered, that the miners realized they'd been washing away incredibly rich silver ore. Two Irishmen, Patrick McLaughlin and Peter O'Riley, hit this ledge of ore at the foot of Sun Mountain, and the boom was on. Henry Comstock claimed prior rights to the ground, and though he soon sold his claims for quick profit and eventually went back to prospecting, his name stayed.

It took another breed of man to develop the Comstock, men like John Mackay, industrious and resourceful, with persistence and good judgment. Mackay joined the rush to Washoe, working in the mines for $4 a day. Fifteen years later, his energy, sharp observation, and quick grasp of opportunity had earned him millions of dollars and the title "Boss of the Comstock."

The mines eventually yielded over $400 million in gold and silver, but they took their toll. The men who worked deep underground were constantly at the edge of human endur-

Early skier Jim Hawkins

ance. Temperatures were often well over 100 degrees, scalding water would burst forth from the rock, and the air became so putrid from rotting timbers and lack of ventilation that a miner could barely keep his candle burning, much less oxygen in his lungs. No ordinary men these, who could push their fears aside and labor daily alongside the perils of such an earthly hell.

Another courageous man was "Snowshoe" Thompson, who braved "the wildest winter storms of the Sierra, carrying the mails strapped upon his back and fearlessly going... where no other man dare venture." For 20 years his fortitude allowed mail service to span the continent through the winters, though it earned him nothing but gratitude and respect. Not that mail service was cheap in those days. The Pony Express charged $5 a half-ounce for letters carried by its daring young riders in 1860. They dashed through the mountains and deserts of central Nevada, changing horses every 15 miles at outposts remotely spotted along the route.

The wilderness was slowly being laid open, and conflict with the Indians was inevitable. The Pyramid Lake War allowed the settlers and the Indians to work vengeance on each other. In the first battle, a loosely organized band of whites from Gold Canyon and Carson Valley were massacred, causing panic throughout the settlements. Three weeks later a force of over 700 men, including troops from California, routed the Indians. Military forts were then set up across Nevada to protect settlers from possible Indian reprisals.

From the outset, the pioneers of Nevada found law and order difficult to maintain. A grand jury instructed to indict citizens guilty of "gambling, concubinage, and other minor

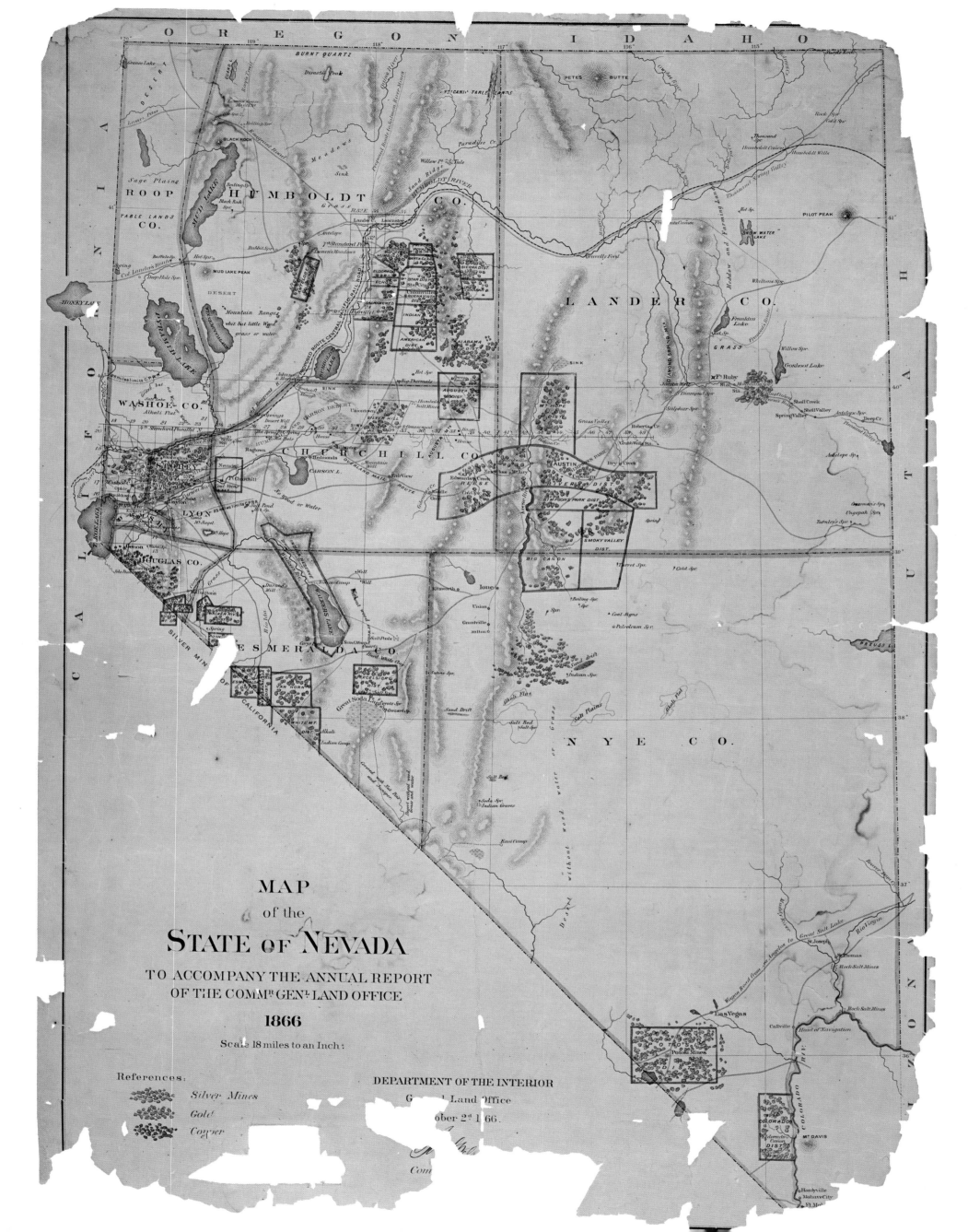

MAP
of the
STATE OF NEVADA

TO ACCOMPANY THE ANNUAL REPORT
OF THE COMM'R GEN'L LAND OFFICE

1866

Scale 18 miles to an Inch:

References:

Silver Mines

Gold

Copper

DEPARTMENT OF THE INTERIOR

Gen'l Land Office

ober 2d 1866.

Com

Carson Valley Ranch

Fort Churchill on the Carson River

Abandoned to the flowers

Virginia City watering hole

Mark Twain

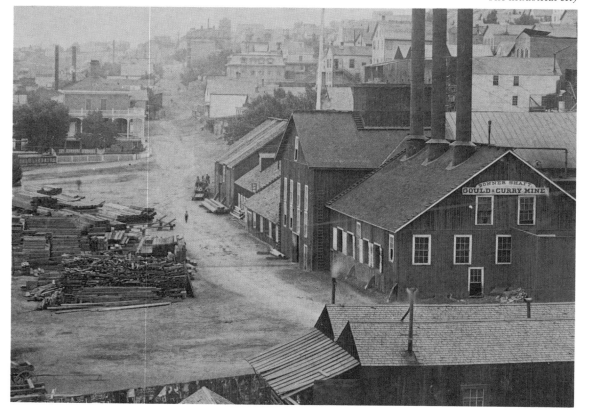

The industrial city

frontier offenses'' adjourned rather than indict themselves. But the press of people coming to the Comstock, coupled with the secession of the southern states, prompted Congress to give Nevada territorial status in 1861. Abraham Lincoln then appointed a former police commissioner of New York, James Nye, to govern the new territory. The "Gray Eagle" was well liked and proved to be an able administrator, molding a firm political foundation out of the chaos in this frontier.

In 1864, when Lincoln needed more Republican strength to assure passage of the anti-slavery amendment, Nevada entered statehood. The wealth of her mines and the votes of her Senators were crucial to the outcome of the Civil War. Her loyalty to the Union is today reflected in the state motto, "All For Our Country," and on the state flag, which bears the words "Battle Born."

The mines not only helped finance the Civil War, and later the railroads and San Francisco; they also created the most dynamic, exciting town in America—Virginia City. At first the clamor and turmoil of thousands seeking easy riches seemed out of place against the peaceful desert hills, but the town took root, and its wide open, pulsating life soon attracted men of talent and vigor who thrived on the intense, fast pace. There was much drinking and gambling, brawling and bawdiness, but Virginia City also offered theater and opera, fine restaurants, reputable schools and churches, and good newspapers. Samuel Clemens, "the most lovable scamp

Dousing the flames, Virginia City

Bower's Mansion

and nuisance who ever blighted Nevada,'' started writing and took his pen name, Mark Twain, while working as a reporter for the *Territorial Enterprise*. What he wrote wasn't always liked, nor always true, but it was always read.

The Comstock fueled a fever of speculation as everyone tried to cash in on the promised bonanza. Legal battles over claim ownership and financial struggles for control of the mines sharpened the instincts and abilities of many men. William Stewart earned distinction as Virginia City's leading attorney and went on to be a major power in the U.S. Senate. Adolph Sutro persevered for 15 years with his idea for a tunnel to ventilate and drain the lowest levels of the mines, and later became mayor of San Francisco.

Through its heyday Virginia City remained a uniquely stimulating blend of industrial city and frontier boom town. Minds and bodies worked with passion to bring the rich ore out of the earth, and that same passion infected every other facet of life. The fainthearted found the free-wheeling independence tolerated in Virginia City intimidating, but for those men and women with more nerve and spirit it was intoxicating. Fortunes were made and lost overnight, opulence was often squandered, and many were swindled; nevertheless, residents shared a camaraderie and goodwill, most noticeable perhaps in the charity shown after the city was swept by fire in 1875.

Fire was a constant threat. Not only were the buildings

Ponderosa pine, Lake Tahoe

mostly wood, but the everpresent wind quickly made a major blaze out of the first few flames. The water supply for Virginia City was often critically short, until 1873 when Hermann Schussler engineered a pipeline to carry water from the Carson Range high above Lake Tahoe down through Washoe Valley and up to the Comstock. The wrought iron pipe was over seven miles long and worked as an inverted siphon: the water gained enough pressure from dropping 2,000 feet into the valley to carry it the 1,500 feet up to Virginia City.

The Comstock also had a seemingly insatiable appetite for timber, which was fed by the enormous stands of ponderosa pine in the mountains around Lake Tahoe. A logging industry developed that scoured the Tahoe Basin clean of timber by the 1880's. Looking around Lake Tahoe today, it's hard to believe that a hundred years ago the mountains were covered with stumps, and that Glenbrook and Incline were roaring sawmill towns. The lumber was floated down to the Carson Valley in flumes that wound around the mountainsides, and was then hauled by train up to the Comstock.

Some of the veins in the Lode were so wide they required a new method of timbering to prevent cave-ins. Philip Deidesheimer devised a honeycomb or square-set method that proved safe no matter how large the ore body was. Eventually over 600 million board feet of lumber went underground to support the mines; today that would be enough to build 60,000 homes!

Charcoal kiln, Eureka County

Forgotten placer flume

For a dry, dusty throat…

Following the discovery of the Comstock Lode, all those dry, bare mountains and canyons throughout Nevada suddenly took on new promise. The restless prospector with his burro and pickax began filtering over the land. The urge to discover the next El Dorado lured these men into every corner of the state. More than anything else, it was the resilience and self-reliance of the early prospectors that opened the rest of Nevada to settlement. Discoveries were made and towns boomed into existence overnight, with names like Austin, Eldorado, Tuscarora, Pioche, Hamilton, Aurora, Eureka. Often the ore body was quickly exhausted and the buildings and streets were left deserted, the tumbleweeds rolling in the moaning wind. Other settlements were luckier when the mines were more productive, or the towns became supply points for new mining districts.

Stagecoaches and freight wagons, trailing long clouds of dust, linked the new communities. It was a rugged experience riding across Nevada in a stagecoach, lurching along hour after hour through the heat and dust. The coaches and drivers were made tough, and they held together through anything. But the passenger was on his own; he was lucky to be getting a ride, even if it meant being tossed around like loose ballast.

Camel caravans were often a surprising sight to travelers. They carried salt to the ore reduction mills at Austin and on the Comstock. Though they were used for several years, the

Truckee River, Reno, 1870's

Stage driver, Tonopah

Hauling water for the railroad crews, Dayton

Bonnelli's Ferry, Colorado River

Pile-driving on the Carson River

Como stamp mill

exotic beasts never really adjusted to the rockiness and alkali of Nevada's deserts, and were despised because they smelled awful and had surly dispositions.

Also a mixed blessing was the coming of the Central Pacific Railroad. Five thousand Chinese laborers pushed the tracks across Nevada in the late 1860's, linking the state with the rest of the nation. Railroad towns like Reno, Winnemucca, and Elko sprouted and grew quickly into major centers of distribution and commerce. But the railroad took over 4,000 square miles in land subsidies along its right-of-way, and once in operation it milked Nevada users heavily. A carload shipped from Reno to New York cost $200 more than the same carload shipped from San Francisco to New York.

New mineral discoveries were often made simply by chance. That was the case when Jim Butler picked up a stone to throw at his straying mule and started the swarm to Tonopah in 1900. In seven years nearby Goldfield had become the largest city in Nevada, with 20,000 souls hustling about. The remoteness of the region and the lack of water and timber didn't stop the promoters from having a field day. They resorted to any strategem to attract publicity—even to holding championship boxing matches in the new mining towns. Speculation reached a feverish intensity throughout the country, and demand for stock in a Nevada gold or silver mine was so contagious that many investors fell victim to unfulfilled claims.

Prospectors near Goldfield, 1903

Tonopah miners, Jim Butler second from left

Tonopah Stock Exchange, 1908

The same free-wheeling, open life-style that marked Virginia City attracted free-spirited, independent people to the booming towns in southern Nevada. The ''anything goes'' atmosphere encouraged union leaders to foment a new radicalism among the mine workers. Forty-five years earlier, miners at Virginia City successfully organized the first labor union in the West, which brought stability to the work force on the Comstock. But in Goldfield, the Industrial Workers of the World demanded a more socialist sharing of the wealth. ''High-grading'' was encouraged, whereby miners walked off shift with millions of dollars worth of high grade ore concealed in their clothing. As the IWW became more radical and violent in its tactics, it started to lose solidarity, and in the end was unable to wrench concessions from the powerful mining companies.

The advent of the automobile provided a novel means of getting around in the desert country. Prospectors found it the quickest way to rush to a new ore discovery and stake a claim. Auto stage companies were soon competing with the railroads and stagecoaches for mail and passenger service. But roads were nonexistent; tracks wandered through the hills and brush, following the line of least resistance. And to jounce along in a car was to be smothered in dust while worrying about whether or not the next breakdown could be repaired.

Though the mining booms came and went across Nevada and were not the most durable economic force, they did lure

Blue sky for sale!

Touring Clark County, 1915

Cosmopolitan Hotel, Belmont

Hot springs baths, Soda Springs

4th of July parade, Tonopah, 1906

A day's work ahead

people into the state, and once here many saw opportunity outside the mines. The country surrounding the mining districts often proved to be excellent rangeland for livestock. Bunch grass and "winter fat" — a type of sage that made good herbage after the first frosts — kept the cattle well fed year-round. That's not to say ranching was easy in Nevada. There were hard winters to contend with, and a scarcity of water; and the range was not as easily renewed as in other places. Cattlemen and sheepmen sometimes failed to find enough elbowroom in the wide expanses of the state and resorted to the frontier justice of a .45 caliber bullet to defend their domains. After the railroads opened Nevada to profitable out-of-state markets, large ranching empires — some extending for over 1,500 square miles — were carved out of the land that was once considered worthless desert. There wasn't much to stop a man who believed "bigger is better."

Agricultural development came quickly on the heels of demand for foodstuffs in Virginia City. A premium was placed on fresh fruits and vegetables, dairy products, and good stock feed. It did not take long for some men to see that cultivating the land could be just as rewarding as tearing it up for gold and silver. The growth of small farms kept pace with the spread of mining across the state. With a little bit of luck the land could be made to produce, if a settler found sufficient water and was willing to invest some of his own sweat.

Since the crucial factor was water, irrigation became a

Range camp

Water on the land, Carson Sink Valley

A good team is still needed.

Building the Truckee canal

15-mule combine, Newlands project

Homesteading near Fallon, 1905

A good try; Newark Valley

necessity. The most ambitious plan involved diverting part of the Truckee River through a 31-mile canal to the Carson River, where it would be stored in a reservoir and then used to turn the Carson Sink Valley into a blooming oasis. Francis Newlands, a Nevada congressman, sponsored the Reclamation Act in Washington, and when it passed, in 1902, the Truckee-Carson Project became the nation's first federal reclamation project. Newcomers rushed to homestead in the valley, but the growing was tough, since the amount of water available had been overestimated and the soil was plagued with alkali.

Yes, almost any way you approached her, Nevada was a tough land to come to grips with. But there were many who were lured by her possibilities; they came and worked in the mines, inhabited the shifting towns, and settled in the lonely valleys. Often life proved too strenuous. Poor judgment or a toilworn spirit signaled defeat, and sometimes it was simply bad luck that forced a man to abandon his dreams or dig a grave for his wife. Nevada was a vast crucible, testing men and women as no other part of the country could. There was a greater risk that you wouldn't make it, but the pride and satisfaction of building an independent livelihood where so many others feared to go was ample reward for those who proved equal to the task. And it was these people who gave Nevada the resourceful, self-reliant and confident character that it maintains to this day.

Ellie and Joe Nay

End of the hardship

Made it! Dixie Valley

The Southern Desert

Nowhere in Nevada did I feel so strongly the stark intensity of the land as in the southern part of the state. Here, the Mohave Desert dictates the nature of existence with a searing harshness. The heat and the wind, the lack of water, the isolation, all work toward making a man feel out of place, as if he's trespassing on ground reserved for a secret destiny in a future millennium. Yet this mysterious austerity also intrigues and fascinates. The imagination is sometimes overwhelmed. I sat watching the sun set over the Eldorado Mountains and imagined I could read a message in a language of shadows. As the sun arcs through the sky, and the mountains and hills are slowly eroded, the shadows change from minute to minute, day after day, always telling the story of time, the earth, and the sun.

Life in the desert is centered on survival. Reduced to such elemental terms, it takes on an elegant simplicity. The chain of life starts with a drop of water absorbed by the roots or seeds of any of a number of desert plants that may have been dormant for months. With what would be a mere trace of rain in other parts of the country, the southern Nevada desert blooms forth with a profusion of wildflowers to rival even California. But the color is short-lived; only those plants that can store the precious water prevail. This arid and apparently desolate land is scattered full with Joshua trees, yucca, creosote bush, mesquite, and an amazing variety of cacti and grasses.

These plants have all adapted to the rigors of the parched land, and provide sustenance to an abundant assortment of animal life. Insects, lizards, and snakes; ground squirrels, rabbits, and kangaroo rats; coyotes, roadrunners, and burros — to name just a few — thrive in the tightly interdependent environment of the desert. Kit foxes are typical, shy and timid and rarely seen during the heat and brightness of day. Their dens are a refuge until the cool of night, when they venture forth to prey upon mice and rabbits and other small creatures scurrying about in the darkness. There is a balance and harmony to life in the desert, an equilibrium both fragile and unforgiving. Every link is crucial: remove or displace one and an irredeemable loss occurs. Yet that same chain of life is constantly consuming itself with an indifference that mocks our distinction between life and death. The desert indulges no excesses, no extravagances; in its elemental simplicity, it achieves a purity that sometimes seems sublime.

But that certainly wasn't what attracted people to the area in the first place, because southern Nevada wasn't a desert 12,000 years ago. It was cooler and wetter, with forests and thick vegetation. At that time prehistoric man inhabited the Tule Springs area north of Las Vegas, and hunted big game: mammoth and ground sloth, elephant and bison. As the climate warmed, people of the desert culture roamed the region as they did the rest of Nevada. But only in southern Nevada did an actual Indian civilization develop. Pueblo Grande de Nevada was the heart of a farming culture along the Virgin and Muddy rivers between 700 and 1100 A.D. These Indians irrigated their land and made a variety of artifacts, including

Joshua tree bloom

Kit fox

Jump cactus, Eldorado Canyon

Abandoned to the sun

Wilfrid Gagnon

pottery and turquoise jewelry; they even mined salt from nearby caves, and carried on trade with other Indian cultures in the Southwest. It was a more peaceful way of life than what the white man brought to Eldorado Canyon in exchange for the gold and silver hidden in the rugged hills.

Although probably first discovered by the Spaniards in 1776, gold in the Eldorado district failed to attract much attention until the 1860's, when a number of claims were made. The community that developed was one of the most frenzied, wild and lawless settlements in the West. The area was so isolated from any seat of authority that it became a haven for every kind of desperado the West could produce. Greed, lust, and violence became the prevailing virtues as murderers, bandits, and thieves worked their havoc and then melted into the desert to avoid capture. Even well into the 20th Century a crazed half-breed eluded capture while he continued to slay prospectors and residents at random.

Today, gentler souls inhabit the Eldorado Mountains. Take Wilfrid Gagnon, who has prospected the hills as a hobby for years. It was a surprise to come around the curve of a narrow, dusty road and meet this gentleman living alone out with the Joshua and mesquite under a hot, hot sun. "When I retired from my body-and-fender work in Las Vegas," he said, "I made eleven claims out here. This one I called the 'Nugget of Gold.' I leased it, so now somebody else is working and developing it, leaving me time to build violins, which is what

Lake Mohave sunrise

Eldorado miners, 1864

I really like to do." He showed us a case with over two dozen beautifully handcrafted violins. Many were of his own unique design and made from native woods. "My goal is to design a violin that makes a better sound." And then he showed us what he meant by playing a five-string instrument that combined features of a violin with those of a viola.

There was a spark to Gagnon's eyes, an ableness and power about him. He was using his life, instead of being used by it. He had a vitality, I thought, that maybe now could flourish in no other place; and later I was surprised to observe the same thing about Las Vegas.

The feverish intensity of gaming and glamour in Las Vegas is a startling contrast with the surrounding desert. Yet Las Vegas seems as appropriate in southern Nevada as it would seem out of place anywhere else. It is an oasis, how-ever different in style from the picture that word usually conjures, and at one time in fact its attractions were far different from those of today. Las Vegas means "the meadows" in Spanish, and in the 1830's and 40's its springs and lush grasses were a welcome relief to muleteers bringing their caravans across the sandy wastes between Santa Fe and southern California. After the Mormons failed to establish a mission at Las Vegas in the 1850's, O.D. Gass, an Eldorado miner, acquired the land and built the Las Vegas Ranch, a bountiful plantation with fields of alfalfa and grain, corn and

Las Vegas from Potosi Mountain

other vegetables, fruit orchards, and even grapes for wine and raisins. But not until the railroad was completed and a townsite laid out in 1905 did Las Vegas begin to take on the appearance it has today. And today it is indisputably the gaming and entertainment capital of the world.

Games of chance have been a fascination for man from time immemorial. Essentially, people gamble for the same reason that they climb mountains or go to the moon; there's a peculiar elation in "bucking the tiger," in achieving something in the face of risk. It was felt by those who staked their lives on settling in Nevada; it is felt by those who gamble in Nevada today. The odds are governed by the laws of probability now, and not so much by the vagaries of land and climate; but the motive remains the same. Many don't bother to calculate the risks, and for them winning or losing is merely a matter of luck, with nothing at stake but a few dollars. But others take their gaming in earnest, assaulting the tables with the same strategy and intensity of purpose they'd give to conquering Mt. Everest. Some make it and some don't. The brightly-lit casino is no less indifferent than the vast stretch of desert outside.

Alien, pitiless that desert may be; but it also offers a special sort of solitude and, to the explorer, not a little astonishment. Just a few miles west of Las Vegas, hidden grottos can be found among the Red Rocks, with pockets of water

Come Lady Luck!

Red Rock Canyon hideaway

Sandstone Bluffs

A frog in the pan is worth...

Ground-mat cholla

Spring snowmelt, Charleston Peak

The desert blooms!

that still yield gold to the pan. The Sandstone Bluffs rising straight from the desert floor reveal eons of geologic history; the gray limestone and shale were deposited at the bottom of a sea 400 million years ago, and the red bands were sand dunes some 150 million years ago.

The Valley of Fire is yet another dramatic landscape, an everchanging play of light and dark across a colossal tumble of stone. As shadows flicker through the orange-red crags, the mind is moved to contemplate how and when such a land could have been formed. An ancient people must also have found the mysterious presence of these rocks fascinating, for they left a wide variety of petroglyphs throughout the area that continue to tantalize our imaginations.

Most surprising in southern Nevada are the Spring Mountains, towering out of the desert to the nearly 12,000-foot summit of Charleston Peak. The sound of aspen leaves dancing in the breeze and the touch of cool mountain air are a delightful shock to a body which just an hour earlier sweltered among the cacti and yucca of the desert.

The Spring Mountains are like an island emerging from the ocean, isolating a microcosm of plant and animal habitats. Six North American Life Zones, from Lower Sonoran with its characteristic desert habitat, all the way to Arctic, are found here. Vegetation ranges from phlox and lichen on the high, exposed slopes to a wide variety of spruce, fir, and pine lower down. Chokecherry and wild strawberry grow

Bull elk in the Spring Mountains

Oopsy-daisy! Lee Canyon ski area

An aspen oasis, Scout Canyon

Landsailing near Las Vegas

among the aspen; still lower, mountain mahogany and oak-brush give way to juniper and piñon pine, and sagebrush. Who would think that elk and wild turkey roam through the forests less than 20 miles from where a desert tortoise chews on beavertail cactus? Or that a skier can enjoy powder snow an hour from Las Vegas? Such variety is achieved by the workings of a delicate balance maintained over a long period of time. I found myself hoping we don't destroy that balance, as I sat at sunset in a grove of ancient bristlecone pine, high on the flank of Charleston Peak, and looked north toward Frenchman's Flat, where the Atomic Energy Commission has been detonating nuclear explosives for 25 years.

In the early 1950's a remote section of southern Nevada was chosen to be the proving grounds for nuclear research in the United States. It has been a mixed blessing. Those involved in the quest to harness atomic energy—whether for weapons, for rocket propulsion, or for digging harbors and canals—are pushing back the frontiers of our own time much as Nevadans did a century earlier. There's challenge and excitement here—and risk. Radioactive fallout was a danger until testing went underground. Although the explosions are now limited to 150 kilotons, whether or not their cumulative effect will result in earthquakes or polluted groundwater remains uncertain. And one can only hope that Nevada doesn't become an accidental graveyard for nuclear waste.

An old prospector, abandoning his burro around the turn

Great Basin rattler

Mound cactus

Big Springs pupfish

Budding cotton, Pahrump Valley

of the century, couldn't have known and probably wouldn't have cared about the problems he was creating for a future generation. Today wild burros have become an accepted and thriving part of the desert landscape, but they are also threatening the existence of desert bighorn sheep, quail, many lizards and small mammals, and even a few plant species. At one time the desert bighorn ranged throughout the southern half of the state. Now they're confined to a few remote mountains and canyons, principally in the huge Desert Game Range, not only because of competition with the wild burros for food and water, but also because of man and his guns.

We have some hard choices to make today about how much we can alter our environment without sacrificing its essential integrity. When groundwater is pumped for irrigation in Ash Meadows or the Amargosa Desert, the very existence of rare desert pupfish is at stake. These little fish are marvels of evolution, having survived for millions of years by rapid adaptation to changes in the environment that extinguished countless other species. Today they are found only in a few hot springs in Ash Meadows and nearby Death Valley. The pupfish was a part of life's diversity long before man, and may harbor secrets of evolutionary survival that we ourselves may someday wish to know.

But alfalfa and feed for livestock are also priorities, as are the cotton and melons grown in Pahrump Valley to the south.

Aristes Ramor, haying, Virgin Valley

It seems the biggest question facing Nevadans in the years ahead will be how best to use their water resources. When the desert is irrigated, it blooms with a startling lushness. Sedan grass grows seven feet high along the Virgin River; six or seven cuttings a year feed dairy herds that have only a few hundred yards to stray before being consumed by the rugged, thirsty wilderness. The contrast is as amazing today as it must have been for those early Spanish explorers who, having trekked across a desolate landscape for days, were delighted by the pure, clean waters of this river they named the Virgin.

Even with the potential of water, making an oasis out of this land was no easy task. The Mormons who initially settled here found they had to fight the river itself. Heavy spring runoff would cause it to flood, washing out dams that had been laboriously constructed; summer brought flash floods that filled the canals with tons of gravel and debris. The settlers battled not only the water, land, and climate, but also isolation, poverty, and disease, particularly malaria. A little cemetery overlooking the fertile Overton Valley is mute testimony to their struggle. Children died young then, and only the vigorous and fit survived while life remained such a chancy thing.

In the 1930's men took steps to eliminate some of the casualties of chance by damming a river. It was no ordinary river—and no ordinary dam. The Colorado had been flooding irrigated lands in the Southwest with the same carelessness

Quail

Virgin River sunrise

with which it carved the Grand Canyon. To harness that turbulence was one of the greatest engineering feats of the century. When completed, Hoover Dam was the largest man-made structure on earth, and impounded waters that formed a lake covering over 200 square miles. Even today, to explore the dam is to be overwhelmed. In the massive scale of the structure, in the reverberating hum of the generators, there's an extraordinary sense of sheer power — the force that fuels the legions of high voltage lines marching out across the desert.

Behind Hoover Dam, Lake Mead reflects many moods throughout the year. It can brood somberly through a cold and blustery winter day, or twinkle with sunlight as a summer waterskier races by its shores. The lake is haven for forms of life much different from those which once dwelled in the desert canyons, now flooded. A wide assortment of fish attracts anglers to the lake, and waterfowl and many species of birds find a pleasant retreat along the shores—not to mention the many people who seek relief from summer heat.

Although for some the southern Nevada desert will always seem oppressive, others—and their numbers seem to be increasing—have come to love the uncluttered tranquility of a boundless sky, the clean fragrance left by a passing thundershower, and the romance of late shadows passing across the land. Perhaps only the initiated can understand what a good place this is to be.

Lake Mead pastels

The Eastern Empire

There's a remoteness to the spread of land across eastern Nevada that seems to be an indulgence, a fast-receding luxury in this day of easy access. The mountains and valleys here, the hills and trees, the old buildings, life itself, take on a precious timelessness that can only be enjoyed far from the concrete activities of modern-day man. It is heartening to discover places that have been overlooked or that have not completely yielded to that omnivorous conceit called progress. An early November morning found me wandering through endless stands of juniper above Clover Valley, listening to a lyrical silence and delighting in the knowledge that the jet planes speeding across the sky high overhead would never land nearby.

Such remoteness can certainly mean isolation and loneliness, but it can also foster a pleasant sense of seclusion and intimacy. Many of the little valleys first settled by the Mormons over 100 years ago still offer refuge from the overpowering vastness that characterizes this countryside.

By the 1860's nearly 40 Mormon families had settled in the meadowlands of Clover Valley, Eagle Valley, and Meadow Valley. Springs and small streams provided water for cultivating the land, and the Saints were able to establish a solid, permanent agricultural community. A townsite was laid out in 1864 and given the name Panaca, from an Indian word meaning "metal."

In general, the Indians were a nuisance to the settlers, continually raiding their cattle herds and even stealing crops. Often a band of Indians would sweep through a just-ripened field of wheat before the farmer could harvest it himself.

Even so, it was an Indian who led William Hamblin, a Mormon missionary, to what became the richest ore deposit in southeastern Nevada. The Panaca Ledge gave rise to the mining town of Pioche. Over 2,000 claims were located in the area, and another rowdy, lawless mining town started booming. It's said there were so many quick-draw artists in Pioche that its cemetery was filled with 75 bodies before anyone had a chance to die of "natural" causes. Nevertheless, the town attracted scores of women and girls bent on tying the knot. The marriage business did so well that by 1876 a group of men formed the Single Men's Protective League, "to protect themselves from the encroachments of the female sex, which of late have become so dangerous that the poor male is getting to be an object of pity."

Other areas also witnessed an onslaught of miners and speculators, most notably up in the White Pine Range, where another Indian-assisted discovery of silver-bearing ore created a mining district teeming with 25,000 souls by 1869. Some of the ore contained almost pure deposits of silver close to the surface, which led to a certain amount of cockiness among those who located good claims. One of the owners of the Eberhardt Mine, on being offered $4 million to sell, replied, "No! When we have taken out enough to pay the national debt then we will talk about selling." (Nevada was filled with some very ambitious men in those days. The national debt was $2½ billion in 1870!) Though it was platted

Early Mormon tabernacle, Clover Valley

Mormon crickets

at an elevation of nearly 8,000 feet and was bitter cold in the winter, the town of Hamilton became a major, if short-lived, metropolis. Stages and freight wagons converged on the city, bringing in all the supplies and refinements demanded by the new-found wealth. There were skating rinks and dance halls; jewelers, breweries, and pawnshops; over 50 general stores; and you could drink in a different bar every day, all summer long. Nearby Treasure City even had its own stock exchange. All this and more sprouted in just a couple of years — and died almost as quickly when the veins of rich ore proved to be shallow.

Today the high, open hillsides and narrow canyons of the White Pine Range only hint of the years when they were besieged by restless and eager men. Surges in mining activity always seem to subside much more quickly than pursuits rooted in the soil. That may be why the farming and ranching legacy brought to this part of Nevada by the Mormon settlers endures with little change, while the mines continue to open and close, flourish and expire.

One feature of the land that has changed only slowly through the centuries is Cathedral Gorge, a chasm delicately etched out of soft, chalky clay. The fluted columns and torn ramparts were fashioned by the slow clawing of erosion

Cathedral Gorge

Lesser scaup

Taking a dip in Ash Springs

Pahranagat Valley

Spelunkers entering Leviathan Cave

Quinn Canyon Range

through eons of time. In some moods the formations seem to belong to another world; an explorer can even imagine he's been transported to Venus or Mars.

In contrast, Pahranagat Valley is very much of this earth. At one time it was used as a hideaway by horse thieves and cattle rustlers who fattened their stolen stock in its meadows. The springs still flow, bringing water to the ranches and cottonwood trees that line the valley today. The Pahranagat lakes at the lower end of the valley serve as a wildlife refuge for flocks of migrating ducks and geese.

Most of the mountain ranges in the eastern part of the state are classed as limestone ranges, formed from the faulting and lifting of an ancient seabed. Since limestone is soluble, rainwater seeping underground slowly dissolves the rock, leaving large caverns and deep passageways. Many of these caves were discovered by pioneers and explorers a century ago, but just as many remain undiscovered or unexplored. Spelunkers delight in climbing to the top of a mountain and then descending deep underground to probe a world that never sees the light of day. Many caves offer nothing but long, twisting passages that can be explored only on hands and knees. Dust that hasn't been disturbed during years of quiet accumulation may billow up and choke off further investigation. But the subterranean world also conceals crystal-pure pools and innumerable formations that have slowly dripped into existence. Stalactites and stalagmites are the most common; calcite dissolved in the water passing through the bedrock is deposited on the ceilings and floors of a cave when the water drops evaporate.

Silent shadows across Garden Valley

Cicada

Old Man Cave, Snake Range

Columbine

Tree frog

Near Timber Creek, Schell Creek Range

Aspen patterns, Kalamazoo Summit

Blue grouse

A wealth of silence remains one of Nevada's most pleasing legacies; to notice the different nuances is always a relaxing diversion. Locked in a cave, the silence broods heavily, indignant at having to absorb the rudely echoing noises. Out in the long, wide valleys, though, the silence becomes more yielding, resting as lightly on the land as the shadows stretching out across the sage. And in the mountains, in the bright sunshine and thin air, the silence is light-hearted and easily abandons itself to the splashing of a stream or the murmuring of wind in the trees.

The Schell Creek Range extends for 120 miles through eastern Nevada, and although not the highest, it is the most characteristic of the limestone ranges found here. In the winter the summits are covered with snow which feeds dozens of small streams spilling over the rocks to the valleys below. Lupine and columbine, asters and poppies, the Indian paintbrush and wild gooseberry cover the hillsides through spring and summer. At the higher elevations, stands of yellow pine, Douglas fir, and Englemann spruce provide a welcome change from the more common juniper and piñon pine. Wildlife is abundant, with mule deer, elk, bobcats, mountain lions, and porcupines, as well as numerous smaller creatures of the wilderness. Even little tree frogs can be found.

Anyone hiking in the Schell Creek or nearby Snake Range can expect to be startled by a blue grouse exploding from the

Lehman Creek, Snake Range

Teresa Lake outfall, Snake Range

Mountain conquest

grass. These mountain birds migrate all over the high country, but in an unexpected way. They spend summers in the foothills and along the streams, feeding on insects, evergreen cones, flowers, and wild berries. By fall they've moved up to the high slopes and end up spending the winters sheltered in fir trees that have an abundant supply of needles for food. When the weather warms in the spring, they fly down to the low country again.

Standing above all the nearby mountains is Wheeler Peak, rising to 13,063 feet in the Snake Range. It is Nevada's second highest mountain, and one of the few in the state which have been carved out by glacial forces. A small, permanent ice field is all that remains of the enormous mass of snow and ice that scoured out the cirque below Wheeler Peak. Today mountain climbers find challenge and exhilaration in exercising the stamina and nerve required to work their way up Wheeler's northeast face. Those of us not quite so stout of heart find stimulation enough in hiking to the high lakes—some over 10,000 feet—tucked away in pockets of the glacial moraine.

Wheeler Peak endures as an indomitable monarch, casting its shadow for miles over the land. It is also home to some living monarchs—the bristlecone pines. Among them are individual trees which survive as the oldest living things on

Northeast face, Wheeler Peak

earth, trees which sprouted as seedlings over 4,000 years ago. They can be found standing like twisted driftwood, clinging to the rocky ground between 10,000 and 12,000 feet. How can anything persist for centuries in such a harsh environment, battered by icy winds, blasted with sand and sleet, and crushed by the weight of drifted snow? Part of the secret lies in their extremely slow growth—sometimes as little as one inch in 100 years. The wood is also very resinous, and doesn't rot in the dry climate of high altitudes. But most important, part of the tree dies in order that a small portion may go on living. A narrow strip of bark may be all that supports the needles and the pinecones that produce seeds from which new trees can grow.

Though mountain lions can be found lurking in the more remote parts of the Snake Range, Nevada's state bird, the mountain bluebird, can be seen and heard almost anywhere in the high country—not only here, but across the state. The mountain bluebird is distinguished by its sky-blue coloring; its song is a high-pitched warbling, not unlike that of a robin.

Many of the meadows in the high country of eastern Nevada, as well as the many valleys, provide good grazing land for sheep and cattle. Wild grasses abound—crested wheat grass, Indian rice grass, June grass, to name a few—and

Mountain lion

Bristlecone pine cone

Spring Valley

Mountain bluebird

Pioneer graveyard

Sage grouse

they all make excellent herbage for livestock. Nevertheless, mining continues to leave the biggest mark on the land. Not mining for the glitter of silver or gold as in the old days, or for the more exotic metals demanded by modern technology, but mining for copper, one of the oldest metals used by man.

Most of the other boom towns in the region had lost their vitality before Ely began to flourish at the turn of the century. A railroad and a reduction plant had to be built before the immense deposits of copper could be worked in earnest, but once they were completed, in 1908, and the steam shovels started digging, the investment proved good. In half a century of on-again, off-again operation, the copper pits west of Ely have yielded over $1 billion worth of copper—more than twice the value of all the ore taken from the Comstock Lode.

Steptoe Valley stretches north of Ely for over 100 miles. It is good habitat for countless sage grouse which bolt out of the expanses of sagebrush unexpectedly—much as the Goshute Indians did more than a century ago when they attacked stagecoaches and stations along the Overland Stage road. During the spring and summer of 1863 the rampant Indians made any travel east of Ruby Valley a perilous journey. Seven of the Overland Company's stations were burned, sixteen of its men were killed, and the company lost over 150 horses.

Rest awhile; Pioche

Weed patterns

Pleasant Valley from the Kern Mountains

Hayrake

Blue flax

Peace was restored only after soldiers from Fort Ruby were called out to retaliate.

To avoid paying the high prices demanded by Mormon farmers in Utah, the Overland Stage Company farmed the Ruby Valley to provision their stations. Over a thousand acres of this fertile, well-watered valley were planted, and by 1865 a hundred men were working the land, harvesting thousands of bushels of barley, oats, potatoes, turnips, carrots, and beets. The success of this first farming effort in northeastern Nevada opened the eyes of many settlers, and it wasn't long before others were hard at work building their own ranching empires at the foot of the Ruby Mountains.

Today the ranches share the valley with multitudes of waterfowl and bird life attracted to the marshes of Ruby Lake. These marshes provide nesting and feeding grounds, or simply resting places, for rare trumpeter swans and sandhill cranes, as well as the more common great blue herons, avocets, ducks and geese. The Ruby Lake Wildlife Refuge protects over 37,000 acres, but is open to good bass and trout fishing, hunting in the fall, and some great bird-watching.

Climbing up into the Ruby Mountains and looking out to the south and east, I couldn't imagine this part of Nevada ever changing very dramatically. The distances will probably always keep it isolated, a refuge from the advancing strides of a busy world.

Ruby Marsh

Greater sandhill crane

The Humboldt Basin

From a distance the Ruby Mountains seem to emerge from the low foothills, shimmering like some far-off Shangri-la. Snowy summits dazzle the eyes in the bright, early-summer sun; the green hillsides and slopes lush with wildflowers beckon the traveler weary of brown, sage-covered hills. Like jewels, high lakes lie sparkling in the mountain meadows, reflecting one of the most abundant sources of water in the state. Indeed, the Rubys are a veritable paradise in a land that was once thought to lack even the slightest essentials of Eden.

The Ruby range is extraordinary in another respect. It's one of the few in Nevada that expose Precambrian rock formed at least a billion years ago. Though the mountains were named for shining red stones found in some of the streambottoms in the late 1840's, the gems turned out to be semiprecious garnets and not rubies. Thus the Ruby Mountains and adjacent valleys were spared the indiscriminate onslaught of a mining boom. Instead, the region was settled by men and women who were seeking not wealth but roots and a livelihood that would endure.

These early homesteaders ran into problems when cattle were brought into the area to feed on native grasses found in the hills and lowlands. Shortly after the Civil War, cattlemen started driving large herds of longhorns from Texas to Nevada to supply the mining towns and the burgeoning markets in California. Nevada proved to be natural grazing range for livestock; not only was the grass nutritious and abundant, but enormous expanses of unoccupied land were available. Enterprising men set about acquiring well-watered tracts along streams and around springs; by controlling access to water, they gained control over a considerable amount of the surrounding country. And since the early ranges were unfenced, the homesteader who found himself surrounded by grazing land was unable to protect his fields of grain from the free-roaming livestock.

By the 1880's much of the Humboldt Basin had become a boundless domain for ranging cattle. Men were piecing together vast ranching empires with the same unfettered determination that moved the earlier pioneers. A few ranches spread north from the Humboldt River all the way into Idaho and Oregon. But nature wasn't as obliging as she first appeared. The winter of 1889-90 blasted the cattle industry with unsuspected fury; the herds were decimated, and by spring many outfits were completely wiped out. The surviving ranchers realized the bounty of the open range was not inexhaustible; they began fencing their lands and storing hay for winter feed.

The spread of cattle altered the landscape with surprising swiftness. Once they were subjected to the nibbling and trampling of livestock, the virgin grasslands lost their former lushness forever. Sagebrush, Russian thistle, rabbit brush, juniper and piñon pine invaded the grazed-over land, giving it the character we see today. Native wildlife was the most affected. Feed for bighorn sheep, antelope, and deer was depleted, and their numbers eventually declined as livestock

Rock climber

Ruby Mountains from the Jiggs Bar

Lamoille Canyon, Ruby Mountains

put continued pressure on the resources of the range. The competition still exists, not only for the grasses, but also for the forbs and browse more common today. Few wildlife species in the area are unaffected. One that is secure is the Himalayan snow partridge, since its habitat is high in the Ruby Mountains, inaccessible to grazing cattle and sheep. These big birds imported from the Hunza province of Pakistan look like giant chukars, and are slowly gaining a foothold in the high country above 9,000 feet.

Another inhabitant of Nevada also came from a distant mountain country. Euzkadi in the Pyrenees Mountains between France and Spain is the Basque homeland. The Basques first settled in Mexico and California along with the Spanish. Although they were not involved in the earliest sheep operations in Nevada, Basque ranchers and herders from California eventually extended their own operations across the border. From then on the sheep industry grew as rapidly as the expanding flocks, and by the 1890's the Basques were the dominant sheepmen of Nevada.

A strong work ethic was one of the cornerstones of Old World Basque society and likewise is what made the Basques successful as sheepherders. They viewed man's moral worth in relation to his success in conquering physical adversity. To

Himalayan snow partridge

Basque sheepherder

have *indarra*, a trait combining physical strength and strength of character, was to be a Basque. It was this heritage, steadfastly maintained far from his homeland, that enabled the Basque herder to endure the extreme hardship and isolation that came with trailing his flock through the hills for months on end. Taking his wages in ewes, the herder would have enough sheep of his own after three or four years to start working for himself. He would then send for and hire a relative from the Old Country, and the cycle would be repeated. Although for years the cattlemen brought pressure against the roving Basque herders and their tramp bands, this system worked well until 1934, when the Taylor Grazing Act officially closed the public lands to herders who possessed no land of their own.

By that time some Basque sheepmen had acquired ranches in Nevada. Others returned to their homeland, but many stayed, entering new occupations and bringing to their work the traditional values that inspired them to excel in whatever they did.

Early Basque ranchers settled in Independence Valley, which is also where Tuscarora flourished. The mining camp was named after a Union gunboat in the Civil War, and was much like Virginia City in its development. Initially placer

Grazing on the hillsides

Festival time

Hay sled, Patsville

Packstring, Jarbidge Mountains

Chow time!

gold was mined, but the town didn't boom until the 1870's, when silver lodes were discovered on the slopes of Mount Blitzen. Chinese workers who had been laid off when railroad construction was completed flocked to Tuscarora. They worked the placer operations with an industriousness unknown to the less persistent white miners. The town prospered much as other mining towns. Freight wagons hauled goods and foodstuffs, mining equipment and whiskey from Elko, a trade and distribution center on the railroad. Wood was scarce, so sagebrush was cut to fuel the mining machinery; eventually the surrounding countryside was completely denuded. With hundreds of Chinese in the area, a separate community developed, a transplanted Chinatown complete with Chinese restaurants and teahouses, gambling halls, opium dens, and even two joss houses.

Though recent discoveries indicate that there is still gold to be found near Tuscarora, the town has had its heyday. The hills have been left to the livestock and the coyotes.

This country in northeastern Nevada is actually not a part of the Great Basin. The rivers here — the Owyhee, the Bruneau, the Jarbidge, and the Salmon Falls — all flow north, contributing their waters to the Snake River in Idaho. The valleys that drain these rivers and the mountains that feed them have become a mecca for the outdoor sportsman. Many reservoirs — some well known, like Wildhorse and those in the Duck Valley Indian Reservation, and others off the beaten

South Fork, Owyhee River

Coyote

track — have become favorite fishing spots. Rainbow trout fatten quickly on the freshwater shrimp and other aquatic life that thrive in these "sagebrush lakes." The Independence and Jarbidge mountains furnish excellent hunting for those willing to pack into the backcountry.

The Jarbidge is a rugged mountain wilderness that the Indians avoided. The name is derived from a Shoshone word, *ja-ha-bich*, meaning "devil." Legend has it that an ogre stalked the Jarbidge Canyon, preying on any Indians that might enter his domain. The inevitable gold discovery shattered the myth, and the high canyon eventually yielded $10 million in gold and silver. The Jarbidge was also the scene of the last stagecoach robbery in the West. On a cold December night in 1916, the stage was held up by a lone bandit who shot the driver and made away with $3,000. The outlaw was soon caught, though, and was quickly convicted of murder and sentenced to prison.

The Jarbidge remains a remote and wild fastness, but it is no longer a place to be avoided. Today its very wildness is its lure. People seek escape and renewal in the natural liveliness of a sparkling mountain stream and by hiking through the high meadows abloom with lupine and balsamroot, blue flax and "mule-ears"— a common name for the wyethia found throughout the high country.

The major physical feature of northern Nevada is the Humboldt River, 275 miles long and the longest stream in the

Lupine and mule ears, Jarbidge Wilderness

Bobcat

state. It was both a godsend and a bitter disappointment to the early pioneers trekking along its course. Without it the emigrants would never have completed the most arduous part of their journey; nevertheless, few were able to conceal their exasperation and discouragement with a river that slowly dwindled away. In the summer of 1850, Margaret Frink made the journey and told in her diaries what the thousands who plodded west faced along the Humboldt:

"The river is the only water to be had, as there are no brooks, springs, or wells in the valley except at the head, where we first came to it. But we had not traveled fifty miles down the stream before we found the water gradually becoming brackish and discolored from the salt and alkali in the soil . . . . The heat is sometimes oppressive. The dust is intolerable. Many wear silk handkerchiefs over their faces; others wear goggles. It is a strange looking army."

It wasn't until "Crocker's pets" pushed the Central Pacific Railroad up through the valley of the Humboldt to connect with the Union Pacific at Promontory Point, Utah, in 1869, that travel along the river lost its difficulties. The railroad men were aggressive and ambitious, using their ingenuity and resources to forge an empire as strong as any in the West. The Chinese construction crews laid rails across

Nevada at an unprecedented rate. With Charles Crocker pressing them on, they laid a record ten miles of track in a single day. One story has it that when a crew laid off work one day, and the foreman said the reason was that it was 120 degrees in the shade, his boss shot back, "What are you doing in the shade?"

The push to finish the line was understandable. The government had offered the railroads 6,400 acres of land and up to $48,000 in loan money per mile of track laid. Alistair Cooke described the meeting at Promontory Point in his *Winning the West:* "The Union Pacific were all dressed up in their finery; and the western company, the Central Pacific, was full of rugged, backcountry toughs, more like the early

pioneers. The historic words used at the time they drove the golden spike were, 'Stand by! We've done praying!' A San Francisco newspaper announced 'The Annexation of the United States.' "

But the railroaders weren't completely ruthless in their drive to lay track and gain government subsidies. As the crews approached Gravelly Ford, they noticed alongside the railroad grade a decaying headboard at the grave of Lucinda Duncan; they erected a white cross to mark what became known as the Maiden's Grave. Years later, when the right-of-way shifted, the railroad moved the grave and the cross to a nearby knoll overlooking the Humboldt River.

From the journal of James Pressley Yager, a Kentuckian

Humboldt River

Railroad safekeeping

who came down the Humboldt in 1863, we learn that Lucinda Duncan was "An old lady the mother & grand mother of a large part of our [wagon] train. She had been sick for several days & night before last she became very ill so much so our train was compelled to lay over yesterday & last night she died. She was pious and beloved by the whole train, relatives and strangers. Her relatives took her death very hard." The entry for the following day reads: "We paid our last debt & respect to the remains of the departed mother. There upon that wild & lonely spot, we left her, untill Gabrel shall sound his trumpt in the last day . . . . A board with the name of the deceased was put up at the head & boulders was laid over the grave to keep wolves from scratching in it."

Maiden's Grave

A back corner of Paradise

Gravelly Ford was a major crossing point on the Humboldt River for emigrant wagons. Just downstream a few miles were the Beowawe geysers, a landmark for the pioneers. Today they still spout their steaming waters skyward, indicating an untapped source of geothermal energy. The temperature of the earth just a few miles below the surface may be as high as 900 degrees. Ordinarily this heat escapes very slowly, but in some places the high temperatures pressurize the underground water and force it to the surface, where it immediately turns to steam. This steam could be harnessed to power electrical generators and provide a renewable, pollution-free source of energy — unlike coal-fired or nuclear power plants.

In the summer of 1863 a party of prospectors exploring north of the Humboldt River found paradise. It was a valley lying below the Santa Rosa Range, rich in black alluvial soil, well watered by the Little Humboldt River, and offering acres of lush meadowland. Though the Indians harassed the settlers for a few years, the area was soon another pocket of agricultural bounty in the dry wilderness of Nevada. Today, Paradise Valley is home to a few cattle outfits and the people who run them, like cowboss Darryl Munson. Darryl spends the summer with his family and crew working cattle through

Paradise Valley

Darryl Munson

Branding time

Dust on a cattle drive

Day's end

Hold 'em tight!

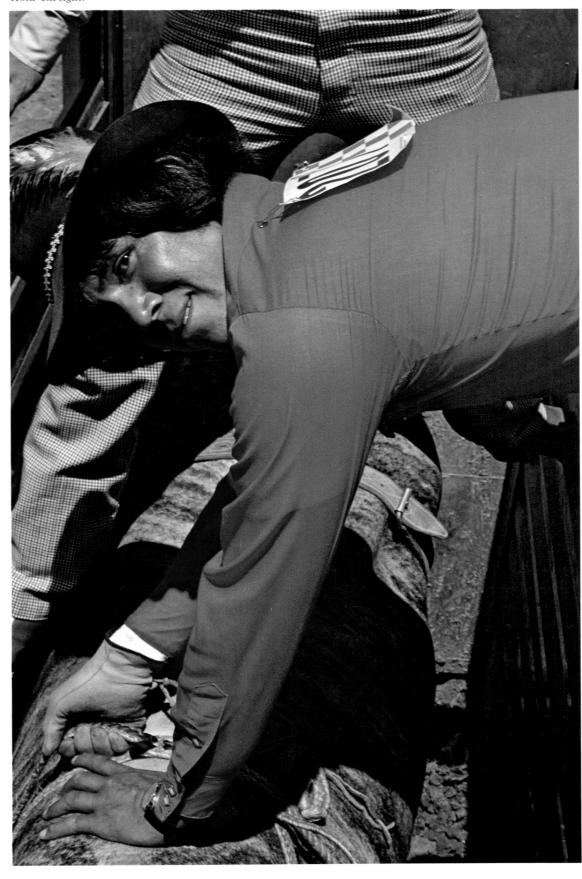

the remote backcountry north of the Valley. His wife is the cook at their isolated trail camp; his son and daughter are part of the crew, riding the hills, moving the cattle all summer long. "It's a good life but lots of hard work," admitted Darryl. "The life of a cowboy is hardly ever dull. There is always something changing, something happening very quickly — day in and day out."

Working every day out in the open country, with its wide and distant vistas, with its lack of distractions, creates a modesty among people that seems all too rare. That modesty is coupled with candor, an easy-going directness between Darryl and his family and the rest of the cowboys at the Three Forks trail camp. They laugh easily and enjoy an honest camaraderie among themselves which fosters a tolerance that doesn't seem to require much patience. There's a simple realness to men like Darryl Munson and the many other cowboys I met in Nevada. They cherish and take pride in living with an independence and self-reliance not found in most other occupations today. Their unpretentious way of life is a valuable heritage, and I believe we do ourselves a disservice by romanticizing their lifestyle, which is still very authentic.

On September 20, 1900, two of the West's most romanticized characters paid a visit to Winnemucca. Butch Cassidy

The ride's over

and the Sundance Kid, after downing a drink in a nearby saloon, called upon a local banker and rode out of town with $33,000. Though a posse quickly gave chase, the pair escaped, and soon left the country for South America.

Today Winnemucca is noted for its russet potatoes. In just a few years deep wells have turned thousands of acres of sagebrush into irrigated cropland. To avoid depleting the soil, the potatoes are rotated with barley, wheat, and hay. The hot days and cold nights here make the Nevada russet potato one of the tastiest in the world. And as long as the wells keep pumping and don't overtax the water resources, the cultivated acres around Winnemucca will keep yielding a generous harvest.

Winnemucca was named in honor of Poito, chief of all the Paiute tribes. He was the son of Chief Truckee, who befriended John C. Frémont and other early white men, thinking the whites were long-lost brothers to his tribe. Apparently Poito earned the name Winnemucca after losing a moccasin while fleeing from the cavalry. The word combines English and Paiute: *mau-cau*, Paiute for "shoe," combined with "one" gives "one-a-mau-cau" or Winnemucca.

Though Poito was a thoughtful and respected leader of his

Water turns sage to barley.

Mourning doves

people and tried to be diplomatic with the white settlers encroaching on Indian lands, it was his daughter, Sarah Winnemucca, who gained the most notice. She received some formal education in California, and dedicated her life to relieving the hapless plight of her people, who were being shuffled about by the often unscrupulous agents of the Indian Affairs Office. Though her efforts failed to bring about any immediate changes in government policy, her lectures in San Francisco and on the east coast during the 1870's and 80's distinguished her as one of the first to publicize the mistreatment suffered by the Indians.

At first glance many of the valleys branching off from the Humboldt seem lifeless, devoid of water — worthless acres spread evenly with sage. But closer inspection and a little exploring always reveal a clump of cottonwoods or a line of Lombardy poplars shading a little spring hidden away in a fold of the hills, beckoning the traveler on any of the dusty backroads of Nevada. Though many have been abandoned, a few are still settled by families who treasure the simple, personal life, the self-sufficiency sustained by such isolation. These green oases stand in welcome contrast to the rest of the land. In one, surrounded by some of the most forlorn looking country in Nevada, a very proud man shared with me peaches from his small orchard, peaches that were the biggest, sweetest, and juiciest I've ever tasted!

Compared with peaches, sagebrush seems pretty worthless. But it really isn't. It's the most prevalent plant in the Humboldt Basin and covers a good portion of the rest of Nevada, which may be why it was chosen as the state emblem and the state flower. The *artemesia tridentata* is actually not related to mint sage at all; it's really part of the wormwood family of plants that includes the familiar ornamental "dusty miller" as well as the culinary herb tarragon.

Sagebrush can be found growing as a low shrub, scattered evenly across a hillside, or in dense stands ten and twelve feet high. Its lushness is always a good indication of rich soil and moisture underground. Since its flowers are so tiny and appear colorless, sagebrush is not often thought of as a flowering plant; at best it's considered today only as browse for livestock and wildlife. But the Indians had many uses for it. They made shelter and clothing from sagebrush, and the leaves were used for medicinal purposes as well, either

Grass Valley reflections

Fruits of desert labor

brewed as a tea, chewed, or pulverized and applied to wounds and sores.

For me the value of sagebrush lies in the tonic effect of its invigorating fragrance after a midsummer thundershower, or in the exhilaration of walking through fields and fields of it on a windy day, being buoyed and lifted as if on the waves of an ocean. And no steak or trout ever tasted better than when broiled over an open sagebrush fire.

Unlike most river drainages, the Humboldt Basin comes to an end at the edge of a desert. Speaking of the river one emigrant observed, "One-half of it sinks into the sand, the other half rises into the sky . . . . The sink of the Humboldt is the end of the most miserable river on the face of the earth." It wasn't quite that bad. Just upstream were big meadows where the wagon trains could rest and cut hay to see their livestock across the desert that lay beyond. (Today the valley here is one of the most fertile in Nevada, irrigated with waters impounded by Rye Patch Dam.)

It was this desert — only 40 miles across — that was the undoing of so many who had come so far. Margaret Frink wrote: "For many weeks we had been accustomed to see property and animals dead or dying. But those scenes were here doubled and trebled. Horses, mules, and oxen, suffering from heat, thirst, and starvation, staggered along until they fell and died on every rod of the way . . . . Around them were strewed yokes, chains, harness, guns, tools, bedding, clothing, cooking utensils, and many other articles, in utter confusion. The owners had left everything, except what provisions they could carry on their backs, and hurried on to save themselves . . . . No one stopped to gaze or to help. The living procession marched steadily onward, giving little heed to the destruction going on, in their own anxiety to reach a place of safety."

The Humboldt Basin is a microcosm of the whole state. It combines all those elements that make Nevada so matchlessly distinctive: the rugged mountain wilderness, the dry, spacious valleys and rolling hills with their hidden pockets of water and green. It is a land that has always been full of challenges, but a land where the personal satisfactions run high. It is home to proud people who have acquired a quiet confidence in themselves — people who have found that life is still fun and good, working close to the earth.

Waves of sage

Forty Mile Desert

The Northwest Uplands

Much of Nevada presents to the eye a relentlessly stark panorama. The first reaction is to view the landscape as awesome, uninhabitable, even intimidating. Yet there's a purity, a simplicity, to everything here, not found where the effects of man's habitation are more apparent. Appreciation of this unadorned country, like so many things in life, is a cultivated trait, and seems to go hand-in-hand with the free-willed living that Nevadans hold so dear.

An early observer of Nevada's geography noticed that "the largest results may be wrought out with the gentlest means." The magnificence of the hills and mountains rising from the desert in the stillness of twilight stand as silent testimony to that truth. The flowing lines of land display a natural elegance far surpassing the designs of any mortal sculptor. At night the sky overflows with stars rising and setting against the sharply etched silhouettes of the earth, and there's an uncluttered beauty, a transcendent grandeur to be found in the distant horizons. No wonder the Indians treasured their homeland and resented the spoiling of it by the white settlers.

Much of the conflict between Indians and whites in Nevada took place in the northwestern part of the state. The Paiutes were basically a peaceful people, but they were eventually provoked as a result of the white man's fear and ignorance. Indian survival had for centuries depended on their reaping a harvest from native food sources. Seeds and pine nuts were mainstays, supplemented by meat from rabbits and an occasional deer or antelope. But the native Nevadans discovered that "the white men cut down our pine trees, their cattle eat our grass, we have no pine nuts, no grass-seed, and we are very hungry." Whereas some of the tribes were willing to follow the ways of the white man in good faith, others, in order to keep from starving, began preying on cattle with the same effectiveness they'd learned stalking wild game. This invited retaliation. By the early 1860's the precedents had been set for ongoing, often indiscriminate warfare.

Black Rock Tom was one of the Indian war chiefs. The *Humboldt Register* reported that he rode "a white horse of extraordinary qualities," and that he "delighted to dally just out of musket range from the white men, caricoling most provokingly, and darting off, occasionally, with the fleetness of the wind ... [taking] great pride in his efforts to 'witch the world with noble horsemanship.'"

The other side had Colonel Charles McDermit, commander of the troops in Nevada, who was killed in an ambush near the Quinn River. He was remembered as "a candid, straightforward, kindhearted man. His men were devoted to him; and the tidings of his death caused tears to well from many a manly eye; and many a man in that little army resolved anew to wreak a fearful vengeance upon the murdering red devils."

The soldiers and the Indians were evenly matched adversaries, and the skirmishing continued. Sarah Winnemucca believed "the only way the cattle-men and farmers get to make money is to start an Indian war, so that the troops may come and buy their beef, cattle, horses, and grain. The

Desert still life

Strawberry roan

settlers get fat by it." A few Paiutes from tribes friendly to the whites eventually turned the tide in favor of the soldiers by helping them scout out and surprise the camps of the defiant, more revengeful Indians. And hostilities slowly subsided as more and more Indians consented to the destiny of living on a reservation.

Today the valleys and high deserts of this part of Nevada lie quiet and still again, with but few surprises. One of these is a gem of an alpine lake, "discovered" as recently as 1959. Blue Lake is a remnant of the glacial epoch in Nevada. Its remoteness — in a cirque atop the Pine Forest Range overlooking the Black Rock Desert — protected it from disturbance for years; an occasional sheepherder and his flock were all that penetrated this hidden sanctuary of the golden eagle, the prairie falcon, deer, antelope, and the mountain lion. As with so many wilderness areas, the land surrounding Blue Lake is fragile, with a delicate balance among the plants and animals found there. Since man so rarely blends into such a balance unobtrusively, he must be careful that his intrusions do not sabotage this wilderness legacy for future generations. Too often it seems the wild areas of this country suffer from an arrogance and thoughtlessness among men — much as the Indians suffered a century ago.

Another surprise is found in the Virgin Valley. It's a forlorn, lonely country, sweltering in the heat of summer and buried under drifting snow in winter; but it's one of those few

Blue Lake, Pine Forest Range

Pronghorn antelope

places in the world that yield the splendidly iridescent fire opal. Unlike other precious stones, opals are non-crystalline, having been formed from layer-by-layer hardening of silica gel over millions of years. They are easily shattered, which makes digging for them an extremely tedious occupation. But their enchanting, even mesmerizing beauty and their rarity make opals among the most sought-after of gem stones.

The Charles Sheldon Antelope Range sprawls across more than half a million acres of northwest Nevada. The gentle contours of this boundlessly empty, treeless land are deceiving. It's not low prairie land but a high plateau, over 5,000 feet. In the absolute stillness of mid-summer, the brightness of the sun is overwhelming. Few people inhabit this country anymore, or travel its roads, and having a flat tire made me acutely aware of this. "What if we have another one?" I kept asking myself. With an unpredictable suddenness, one of the greatest conveniences of 20th-century man can be rendered utterly useless.

We discovered a pile of rocks on a slope overlooking the Range, and were unable to decide why it was made. Many of these cairns are found throughout the West; they might simply be boundary markers, or rocks piled by some early sheepherder breaking the tedium of endless wandering. Early Indians often piled rocks in distant places as part of a puberty ritual, or thought of cairns as shrines for spirits and would add

Chukar

a rock as a token when they passed by.

The Antelope Range is a refuge today for the pronghorn, a distinct Western American species — *Antilocapra americana.* Two characteristics separate the pronghorn from the antelope of Asia and Africa: its branched or pronged horns, and the annual shedding of the hard outer shell of the horns. It is a small creature, weighing around 100 pounds and not over four feet high. Pronghorns seem to delight in running across the wide open spaces, often reaching speeds of fifty and sixty miles per hour. Though unabashedly curious, they are shy and skittish and keep their distance. With their large eyes and phenomenal vision, pronghorns have no difficulty watching your every move from half a mile away.

Another exceptional feature of the pronghorn is its coat. Air cells encased in each strand of hair protect the antelope from extreme heat and cold. The animal can control whether the hair lies flat, providing layers of warm insulation in winter, or stands up, allowing air circulation next to the skin in hot weather. And when the pronghorn is alarmed, the white hairs on its rump stand erect, a signal that can be seen for miles by others of its kind.

The chukar, which was introduced into Nevada in 1935, has come to be the ranking upland game bird in the state. Though not as numerous as in earlier years, these birds still present good sport to hunters willing to pursue them. Chu-

Above Long Valley

Charles Sheldon Antelope Range

Hap Hapeood and Don Erquihea

kars have a nasty habit of running uphill; and when, having climbed after them, a hunter finally flushes the birds, they immediately fly to the bottom of the hill, and the chase starts all over again. My weary legs have reminded me many times that hunting chukars is some of the best exercise around!

Though most of this corner of Nevada remains uninhabited, except for roaming livestock and the wildlife, a few people have found their place here. Hap Hapeood grew up on the Last Chance Ranch back in the thirties, before it was purchased for the antelope refuge. His grandfather homesteaded in nearby Long Valley over 100 years ago, making Hap a third-generation Nevadan. He's close to this land, knows it well, and feels right at home under its wide, wide sky. Hap rarely finds a need to leave this country, and when he does, returning is always a relief. "The isolation grows on you after awhile," he said. "I like the privacy." He talked of the satisfactions of his life: being with his family, working hard, a good meal, a warm fire when you're sleeping out at night, the sun rising on a frosty morning. He seemed pretty happy with his simple life—one in which few things were taken for granted.

Pyramid Lake has been around for a long time, but it's hard to imagine anyone taking it for granted. An unmistak-

Last Chance Ranch

able *presence* pervades the lake and the tufa formations looming along its shore. The many moods of Pyramid Lake seem palpable, changing with an unaccountable spontaneity.

According to Paiute legend the lake was formed by the tears of the great Indian mother of their people. She wept because her sons would not stop battling with each other. Her tears have long since ceased, apparently, and the lake is slowly drying up. In 1905, water from the Truckee River, Pyramid Lake's major inflow, was diverted to the Carson River for the Newlands irrigation project. Since then the level of the lake has dropped over 75 feet, jeopardizing, among other things, the largest white pelican rookery in the United States. If the water level continues to drop, as more water evaporates than enters the lake, the nesting pelicans on Anaho Island will no longer be protected from predators on the mainland, now separated from the island by only 300 feet of water.

The island was named after Anaho Bay on Nuku Hiva, an island of the Marquesas group in the South Pacific. In the spring, several thousand pelicans migrate to Anaho from their wintering grounds in Mexico and Central America. During the summer, while the young birds are maturing, the adult pelicans — with wingspans from eight to ten feet — can

Pelicans, Anaho Island

Pyramid Lake dunes

Fishing, mouth of Truckee River

be seen gliding just inches above the water or majestically high in the sky on thermals that surround the lake.

Pyramid Lake was once known as an incomparable fishing resource. In one season, 1888-89, over 100 tons of the big Lahontan cutthroats were harvested. Sportsmen flocked to the lake, hoping to land one of these record-sized trout, which could weigh up to 40 pounds. And the lake's bounty continued to renew itself — until the flow of the Truckee River diminished and prevented the trout from reaching their spawning grounds. Their numbers slowly dwindled, and by the 1940's few remained in the lake.

Fortunately the Lahontan cutthroat survived, still spawning in other waters of the state. The trout found in Summit Lake and its inflow, Mahogany Creek, have provided eggs for the restocking of Pyramid Lake, which possibly will one day recapture its former place among angling waters of the world.

Surprisingly, Nevada may have more endangered fish species in its waters than any other state. The Cui-ui, a relic from prehistoric Lake Lahontan, suffered decline along with the Lahontan cutthroat. But the fish were able to continue spawning along the shore of the lake or on the sandbars at the mouth of the river, and the Indians still catch them with snag hooks. The red-banded cutthroat is also unique to Nevada

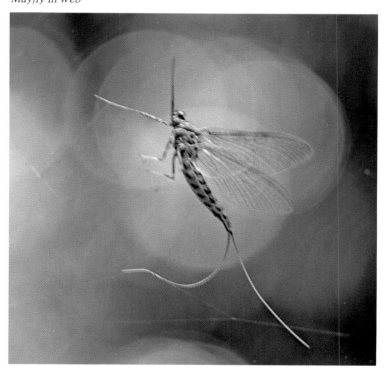

Lahontan cutthroat, Mahogany Creek

Black Rock Desert

and is the only trout that can withstand water temperatures up to 80 degrees. Often the springs and streams around the state will contain various killifish and dace — small minnow-like fish that have evolved into distinct species in their isolated waters. They remain perpetually endangered because their habitats and populations are so small. The existence and survival of all these fish in defiance of the desert is one of nature's impressive contradictions.

"We were evidently on the verge of the desert which had been reported to us; and the appearance of the country was so forbidding that I was afraid to enter it." Many others since John C. Frémont have been intimidated by Black Rock Desert. Emigrants hoping to avoid the hardships of the Forty Mile Desert followed tracks that left the Humboldt River at the Applegate cutoff, and soon found themselves facing a stretch of desolation equal to any in the West — a grey-white, oven-baked playa shimmering with heat waves and forever receding mirages.

Nearly a hundred miles long and up to twenty miles wide, this alkali plain is the epitome of barrenness. Renegade Indians easily eluded soldiers in the inhospitable mountains bordering the desert. The Black Rock Desert is still more remote and forbidding than any other place in Nevada; some ranchers in the area have to drive thirty miles to Gerlach just to get to a phone. After a heavy rain, or when the Quinn River

Turkey vulture

Winnemucca Lake shadows

Indian paintbrush

flows heavily, the playa can be covered for miles by a lake only inches deep. The water, of course, quickly evaporates, leaving the unworldly starkness of the desert unchanged.

The power of evaporation is awesome. At the turn of the century, Winnemucca Lake was 25 miles long and 85 feet deep in some places; boats sailed the lake, and the fishing was comparable to that in nearby Pyramid Lake. Today, with the water no longer overflowing from Pyramid, Winnemucca Lake is an empty basin, a playground for whirling dust devils.

Northwestern Nevada is certainly a hard and rugged country, and no one could say that it appeals to everyone or even to very many. But I'm sure that for those who are lured to explore or live in this country, one of its best qualities is the lack of people. The emptiness is like being out in the middle of the ocean; our senses are sharpened, our awareness quickened, and the freedom from distraction allows a fresh appreciation for living. A turkey vulture soaring in the sky, a natural spray of Indian paintbrush, a patch of shade to sit in, the coolness of a drop of sweat evaporating — it's good that these things should be noticed, not taken for granted. It's good to be reminded that our place in the scheme of things may be less significant than we suppose.

Washoe sunset

The Sierra Front

The Sierra Nevada mountains spilling into the western edge of Nevada were the last obstacle facing emigrants to California. They are also the major barrier preventing moisture-laden Pacific storms from reaching the thirsty lands of the Great Basin. Water is trapped and held in the phenomenal snowfalls that accumulate in the Sierras during some winters. Only a small portion of this resource discharges east, mostly in the flows of the Truckee, Carson, and Walker rivers that give this region the most ample watershed in the state.

The Sierras provide a sharp contrast with mountains in the rest of Nevada. Instead of piñon pine and juniper, the Sierras support tall, cool stands of yellow pine and Douglas fir. Snow plants push up through the humus of pine needles soon after the snow melts. These red flowers are unique in that they lack chlorophyll and are nourished entirely by decaying material in the soil. They're translucent and glow with a fiery brilliance when spotlighted by a shaft of sunlight. The timber was all logged off once, but the forests that have grown back are now valued more for the protection they give to the watershed and for the outdoor recreation they make available, than for the number of board feet per acre they provide.

Marlette Lake was a primary resource for a system devised to use the water supply of the Sierras. An intricate fluming and tunnel system was built in the Carson Range during the 1870's and 80's to bring water from the lake to the siphons that supplied Virginia City. The system is still working a hundred years later. The water of the Sierras was also used to transport timber, either in long flumes winding out of the mountains, or in log drives down the Carson River in the spring. Flow from the Carson also powered a number of mills — both sawmills and mills that stamped and reduced the enormous quantities of ore from the Comstock.

But the waters of the Carson River — so named to honor Kit Carson, Frémont's guide throughout his Nevada explorations — were probably valued most in earlier years by those who slogged through the sand of the Forty Mile Desert and came to the river at what was known as Ragtown. Having exhausted the last of their water out in the desert, the sight of distant cottonwoods would send the emigrants and their remaining stock stampeding to the stream. Its cool waters so relieved the weary, dusty travelers that many stayed for a few days, resting and washing the dust from their now-ragged clothes.

As they approached the foot of the Sierras, some of the pioneers noticed the lush, well-watered grasslands and chose to settle east of the mountains rather than struggle up over them to California. The Mormons also came, colonizing what was then the western part of Utah Territory. By the mid-1850's, a stable agricultural community began to take root all along the front — in Washoe Valley, Eagle Valley, and Carson Valley. All the early farms and ranches thrived on the commerce provided by emigrants following the Carson River route to California, not only selling foodstuffs, beef, and livestock feed, but also providing way stations for the travelers.

Marlette Lake

Solitude in the Sierras

Badger

Grass textures

A party of Mormons led by Judge Orson Hyde arrived in Carson Valley in 1855 with the purpose of organizing Carson County. They established landholdings and set about their work with the industriousness and thoroughness that characterized all early Mormon settlements. A sawmill was built to provide good lumber for buildings. Irrigation ditches were constructed to make the land more arable. A townsite named Genoa, the first in the state, was laid out around the trading post at Mormon Station. Political organization followed and attempts were made to provide consistent enforcement of law and order in this isolated frontier. Many of the non-Mormon settlers resented domination by the Mormons, and were very happy to see them go, two years later, when Brigham Young called his disciples back to Salt Lake City.

The community languished for a few years after the Mormons left. Traffic on the California road dwindled, and many turned to the placer mining in nearby Gold Canyon. But the "rush to Washoe," with the discovery of the Comstock Lode, spurred a resurgence in agriculture in the valleys at the foot of the Sierras; it provided the impetus for widescale settlement by those who built farms and ranches that have continued operation to this day. Every tillable acre of land was put into production. Not only were crops planted and livestock raised, but dairy herds were also brought in. Carson Valley became renowned for the richness and quality of its butter. For many years one distinction of the Palace Hotel in San Francisco was that it served butter only from the Carson Valley.

One of the early dairy farmers here was G. W. G. Ferris,

who brought his family west from Illinois in 1864. He introduced a great number of shade and ornamental trees to the valley, such as hickory, black walnut, butternut, chestnut, hard and soft maple, and many other varieties. He was also the father of George Washington Gale Ferris, who left the Carson Valley and earned acclaim as an engineer and builder of bridges, and as the inventor of the Ferris wheel.

Carson City took root in Eagle Valley after Abraham Curry had difficulty buying a lot in the new town of Genoa in 1858. The *Nevada Tribune* reported: "Curry…examined the townsite [Genoa], and soon selected a corner lot to build upon. The price, $1,000, and no less, must be paid. One of the partners plead for reduction, the other was unflinching in his demands for the sum, or no sale.…Our hero replied, 'Well, then, I will build a city of my own,'…and, before the sun had settled into the lap of the west, Abram Curry was in Eagle Valley for the purpose of redeeming his promise."

In fact, with three partners Curry did purchase the Eagle Ranch and soon had a townsite surveyed. He gave away lots to everyone who would agree to build, "and some were traded off for almost anything that was necessary and obtainable. For instance, the Methodist Church block and the next one south were sold for twenty-five dollars and a pair of boots." With shrewd foresight, Curry left a plaza in the center of town for the state capitol. His efforts were rewarded when the county seat was moved from Genoa to Carson City early in 1861, paving the way for Carson City's selection as territorial and later state capital of Nevada.

Lying less than fifteen miles west of Carson City and about 1,500 feet higher is Lake Tahoe, one of the largest alpine lakes in the world, even though the grandeur of the surrounding mountains make it look much smaller than its 193 square

Washoe Valley

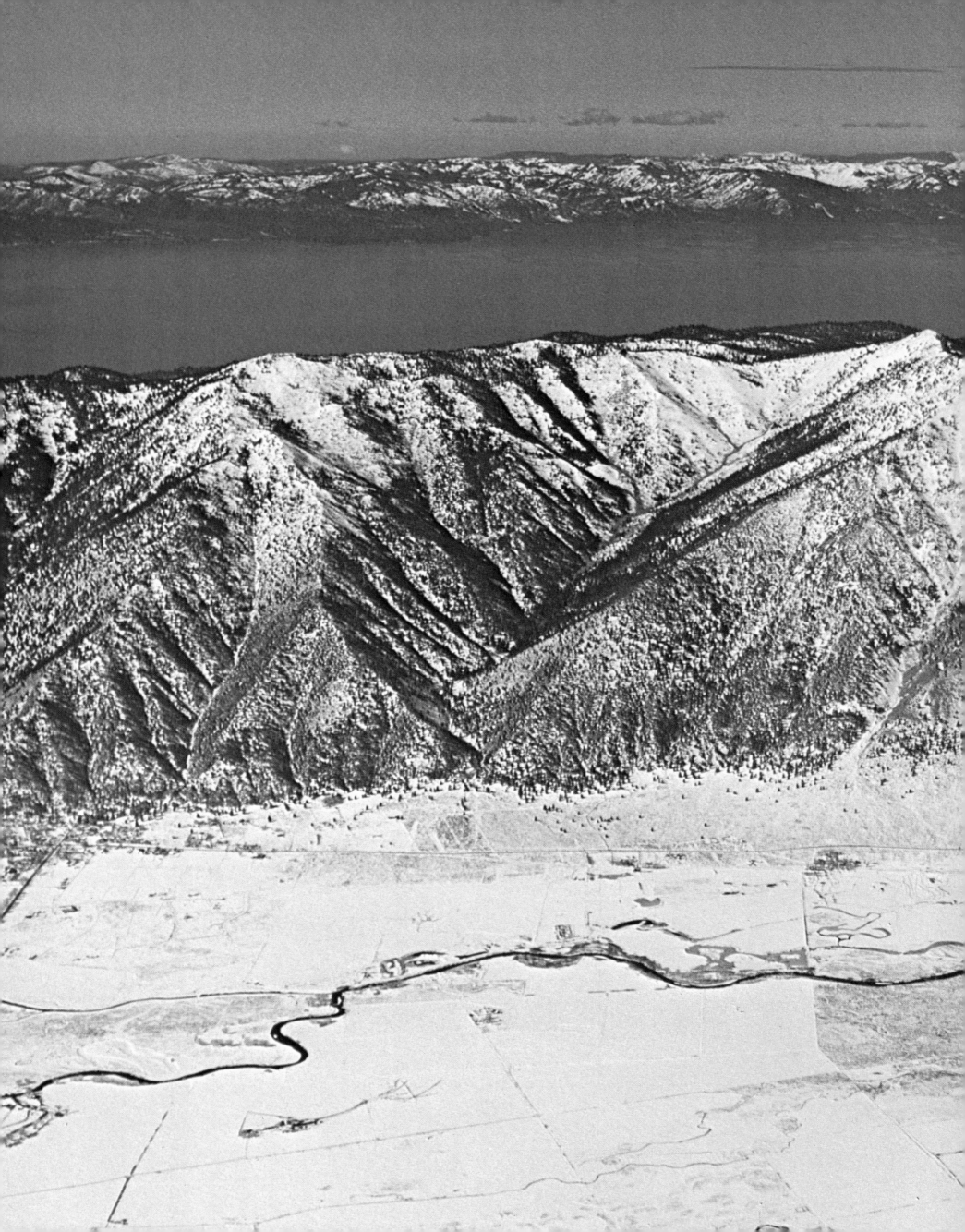

Skiing Mount Rose

mile area. The word "Tahoe" derives from a Washoe Indian word meaning "big water." Though its surface is well above the valleys to the east, the bottom of the lake is actually nearly a hundred feet below the level of Carson Valley. This depth gives Lake Tahoe its enormous volume — almost four times that of Lake Mead. Snow runoff is the primary source of water for the lake and its outflow, the Truckee River. But evaporation in the dry mountain air actually consumes more water than flows out the Truckee — over a million tons of water evaporate from the lake each day!

The "Gem of the Sierras" has been an attraction ever since travelers started coming back over the mountains to Virginia City. Villages and resorts sprang up along its shores, and boats were soon steaming around the lake. It provided a delightful retreat from the summer heat and dust in the valleys — just as it does today. People also followed Snowshoe Thompson's lead and found that the mountains around Lake Tahoe offered recreation in the winter, too. The consequences are proving to be ironic, however: The pristine beauty of the Tahoe Basin is what attracts people in ever increasing numbers, but their impact is starting to jeopardize much of Lake Tahoe's primary appeal — cool, clean air, pure waters, and the quiet seclusion of the forest. The encroachments are happening so gradually and so piecemeal — and are making Tahoe look more and more like any other place — that the effects are easily ignored. But the consequences

Climbing above Lake Tahoe

Ski touring, Tahoe Basin

Winter portrait

Hang gliding above Peavine Mountain

Sailing on Lake Tahoe

Truckee River tuber

accumulate, and without more foresight the lake may slowly lose the distinction it received from Mark Twain as "the fairest picture the whole world affords."

Controversy has surrounded Lake Tahoe ever since Nevada and California fought over water rights to the lake early in this century. The outcome was that California was not allowed to drain the lake for irrigating the Sacramento Valley; at the same time flow in the Truckee River was regulated to prevent the lake level from rising in the spring and flooding shoreside developments, and then lowering in the fall, leaving them high and dry.

The Truckee River has been called "the lifeline of northern Nevada." Its waters supply the Truckee Meadows and provide precious irrigation for the farms and ranches around Fallon. Some dams on the river have generated hydroelectric power for 75 years. In earlier times the river was a pathway for pioneers, leading them up into the Sierras. The misfortunes of the Donner party, trapped in early snows, were unique, but did not keep others from using this passage over the mountains. The Central Pacific Railroad used the Truckee River route for laying its rails. The town of Verdi, named by railroad officials for the Italian opera composer, was established along the river to supply railroad ties, and shortly after the railroad was completed, Verdi was the scene of the first train robbery in the West. Late on a November night in 1870, just outside of town, seven men boarded an east-bound train, disconnected

"Gone but not forgotten…"

Downtown Dayton

the passenger cars, and obliged the engineer to continue down the track a way before they stopped and broke open the Wells Fargo strongbox in the express car. They seized $41,000 in gold coin — payroll for the Yellow Jacket Mine on the Comstock — and slipped away into the night. They were caught and brought to justice, and at the trial one of the robbers complained that he'd been practically *forced* into train robbery by all the extra protection Wells Fargo was giving to its stagecoaches.

The railroad also gave impetus to the founding of Reno. In 1868 a man named Myron Lake deeded some of the land around his toll bridge and wayside inn to the railroad in return for a promised station. After the first train arrived, the town burst into activity as the major transshipment point for freight and passengers on their way to Virginia City or any of the other mining towns scattering around the state. Today Reno is still a major distribution center, not only for much of Nevada but for the entire West Coast. It's also home to some of the most vigorously outdoor-oriented people in the West. The recreational opportunities here are unlimited, with the desert country stretching away to the east and the mountains and lakes to the west.

Reno was also the first to capitalize on legalized gambling in the state. It wasn't always legal. Nevada's first territorial legislature passed an act prohibiting games of chance, after Governor Nye proclaimed that gambling was one of the

Matthew Ajo

worst of vices. "It captivates and ensnares the young," he declared, "and blunts all the moral sensibilities and ends in utter ruin." In subsequent years the legislature intermittently legalized and prohibited gambling in the state, which had little effect on its popularity or practice. In 1931 the solons decided what was being done secretly could be done openly and could become a source of revenue for the state. (Interestingly enough, New York, California, Florida, Illinois, and New Jersey actually collect more revenue from gambling than Nevada, mostly from para-mutual betting.) Today gambling revenue provides nearly 80 percent of Nevada's state budget.

Though there's resurging excitement about Nevada's modern growth potential, the old ways haven't disappeared. One who helped keep them alive was Lucius Beebe, who worked to restore Virginia City's early flavor and revived the famous *Territorial Enterprise* newspaper. He also battled the phone company's efforts to make Nevada the first all-dial state. "With dial," he said, "you can find out what time it is; but you still have to get an operator to find out what day it is."

Lucius Beebe is dead, but there are still people like George and Matthew Ajo to maintain the frontier values. The Ajo brothers have been prospecting around the state for an untold number of years. I found them living in a couple of shacks out near Whiskey Flat. Even all alone out in the desert, they live separately — Matthew drinks and George doesn't.

Jackrabbit

I asked George how he knew where to place a claim. "Well," he said, "first of all you have to take the time to get on a first-name basis with the rocks. That takes years, you know. Then they start talking to you." George and Matthew had worked a cut into the sloping hill, exposing "some pretty good grade copper ore. We hope to get a bigger outfit to come in and lease it. Then we'll move on and work on another claim. We've got to do so much work on every claim. It's just like a hobby. Something that keeps your mind open and alert. Although I have another hobby — I do oil painting and portrait work, but that's when the winter gets rough."

The Ajo brothers weren't too far from Aurora, site of the first important mining discovery after the Comstock. For a while in the early 1860's it looked like Aurora's mines would be even more prosperous than those in the rival mining district at Virginia City. But by 1869 the surface bonanzas were exhausted and the town declined. During its heyday, Aurora was claimed by both California and Nevada, and became the seat for two separate counties, Mono and Esmeralda. Aurora residents enjoyed having two county courts and electing two slates of officers, and at one time the legislatures of California and Nevada were both presided over by men elected from Aurora. The dispute was finally settled

Sweetwater Creek

when the state line was resurveyed and the boundary fixed four miles west of town.

Aurora also witnessed a jailbreak by the legendary stage-coach robber Milton Sharp, who fancied himself a latter-day Robin Hood. He was very effective at lightening the load on some of the Wells Fargo stagecoaches, and supposedly shared his take with some of the more destitute residents of the area.

Another legend in his own time was Jack Wilson, a Paiute Indian who lived along the Walker River in Mason Valley and was known as "Wovoka" to his people. He was raised by a white family, and from them learned of the Bible's teachings. Apparently, a revelation from God allowed Wovoka to become a prophet to his people, and he was revered by Indian tribes across the nation as their messiah. He advocated a universal peace among all mankind, and told the Indians that they "must be good and love one another, have no quarreling, and live in peace with the whites … must work, and not lie or steal … must put away all the old practices that savored of war;" that, if they faithfully obeyed his instructions, they would at last "be reunited with the friends in this other world, where there would be no more death or sickness or old age." He gave the Indians hope for the future, a vision that their plight would someday improve.

Wovoka also introduced the Ghost Dance, whereby participants would chant for hours and hours while clasping hands and circling in a slow shuffle. They hoped to hasten the

Ready for the parade

day when the Indians could abandon their poverty. Some tribes, notably the warlike Sioux and Cheyenne, misinterpreted the dance as a way to remove the white man from the face of the land, which invited the government to move in and quell what had become a major religious movement.

The Paiutes no longer practice the Ghost Dance, but they do still congregate. For a few days every summer Fallon teems with Indians from tribes across the country who come to participate in the All-Indian Rodeo. While the young men bite the dust in the arena, the older tribe members sit in the shade for hours, playing the age-old hand game. The players sonorously chant and beat sticks to distract their opponents from noticing the movement of a stone marker passing from hand to hand. At a signal, the leader of the opposing team guesses which hand holds the marker; if he is correct, his side wins a counter and gets to conceal the marker on the next round of play.

Fallon grew with the hopes of those attracted to the Carson Sink Valley when the Truckee-Carson or Newlands project was completed. The water was to irrigate 350,000 acres, but after the dams and canals were built and the water arrived, the farmers realized the soil was too heavily laden with alkali and salts to support the diversified agriculture they had planned. Instead, the water had to be used initially to leach the minerals from the soil. Productive land was created, though the amount of farm acreage is considerably less than originally anticipated, and today "Hearts of Gold" cantaloupe are grown here, as well as alfalfa and other kinds of livestock feed.

"The ultimate purpose is to afford the world an object lesson of successful cooperation, both in community life and in the life of a great commonwealth of the United States, in

Sunflower

Sunset near Carson Sink

Overleaf: *Sand Mountain*

Hunting at Stillwater

Canvasback

order that demonstration may disarm criticism and help to lift the world to better living." Such was the appeal that attracted scores of hopeful people to a socialist colony founded east of Fallon in 1916. Nevada City was the fountainhead for an ambitious movement that promised to convert Nevada and the rest of the West to the tenets of socialism. In contrast to the "every man for himself" philosophy held by so many settlers, Nevada City represented a way of life that formally recognized man's interdependence. It attracted all kinds of people: utopians, pacifists alarmed by World War I, Marxists and populists angry at American social organization, as well as many who simply were unable to survive the hardships and loneliness of the frontier on their own. It was an attractive scheme, but the colony tried to encompass too many diverging beliefs and ideas. After a couple of years it succumbed to anarchy; the promoters had gone broke, and the surrounding citizenry became enraged when the county sheriff was killed by a draft evader.

Though most of the Carson River's water is used for irrigation, some of it eventually spills out into the Carson Sink, forming a tule marsh for waterfowl and waterfowl hunters. Contrary to what might be expected, the water does not sink here; the groundwater level is so close to the surface

that water is lost only to evaporation. In some winters Stillwater is home to over 35,000 canvasbacks.

Another feature of the land left over from the days when Lake Lahontan covered this low country is Sand Mountain. What was once probably part of a huge beach has been transformed into a restlessly shifting dune. Its flowing lines and shadows are constantly reworked and reshaped by dry winds that blow across the Carson Desert. The dryness of the sand and the steepness of the slopes are two reasons given for the eerie singing or groaning that breaks the desert stillness as the sand blows and tumbles over itself. Attempts to use the sand have failed, and the mountain has been left to its destiny: clay for the sculpturing of the wind, and a playground for those who venture up its slopes.

Sand may not seem strange in the desert, but I never cease to be amazed when I find seagulls far from the ocean. They abound at Walker Lake, which like Pyramid Lake is a catch basin that evaporates water draining from the Sierras. Gulls aren't really restricted to coastal waters; various species actually migrate all over the West. Nevertheless, they still seem out of place wheeling along the shore of Walker Lake with the snows of Mount Grant in the background.

The watershed of the Sierra Front makes this region one of the most diverse in Nevada. It is a corner that contrasts in many ways with the rest of the state, but it is also where much of the unique character that is Nevada's heritage first took root. Openness, candor, friendliness — values that have taken such a battering elsewhere — still flourish here, along with and because of the individual freedom that Nevadans are so willing to preserve.

Collared lizard

The Mountain Heartland

The vast open space found in so much of Nevada belies the essentially mountainous character of the state. To fly over Nevada is to see range after range cresting up from the valley floors like waves rolling out across the ocean. These ragged peaks give the land much of its grandeur and variety. They're covered with snow through winter and spring, and the state's name is taken from this fact — *nevada* is a Spanish word meaning "snowcapped." Without the mountains and the snow, Nevada would indeed be a barren, fruitless desert. Instead, snowmelt creates many of Nevada's secrets: the hidden streams and canyons, springs and high meadows. Melting snow recharges the groundwater used to irrigate the fertile desert soils. And it was snow runoff that washed the hills and exposed veins of ore for the wandering prospectors to discover.

Over 300 distinct mountain ranges have been identified in Nevada; they include a wide variety of types — granite ranges, volcanic, sandstone, limestone, and metamorphic ranges, as well as numerous composite types. Many of them are still on the rise, as evidenced by the earthquakes and faulting that continue to occur. Nevada averages eight earthquakes a day. Most are insignificant, but as recently as 1954 a quake registering 7.3 on the Richter scale slashed open a fault line stretching for miles along the slope above Dixie Valley. In some places the mountain rose as much as 15 feet.

One of the most representative ranges in Nevada is the Toiyabe, stretching for 120 miles through the central part of the state. The Shoshone Indians first called the heights looming above them *biatoyavi*, or "big mountains." The range is a fault block sloping up from the west, with a steep scarp on the east. Huge masses of granite form cliffs and spires that beckon the rock climber, while other portions of the range expose a jumble of volcanic rock or sharply eroded sedimentary deposits. The high snowfields feed countless streams that cut steep canyons and water narrow valleys lined with cottonwoods and aspen. To the east the dusty expanse of the Big Smokey Valley swallows up any and all water spilling out from the foothills.

Much of this mountainous country is still subject to mineral exploration. The landforms are raw and not hidden under layers of soil and vegetation, so the geology is more evident and more accessible than in other mineral-bearing regions. Modern-day prospectors have found deposits of lithium, barite, magnesite, mercury, gypsum, borax, beryllium, and tungsten — to name just a few of the metals and minerals that are being taken from the ground in Nevada today. Whereas the earlier prospectors confined their search to locating surface traces, and began mining only when high-grade ore was discovered, today large low-grade deposits, amenable to open-pit mining, are located with extensive drilling operations. But that's not to say Nevada has become solely a province for the big mining outfits. Many of the small, older mines are still being worked for a profit — depending on the fluctuating price of gold or silver.

There was mining activity in Kingston Canyon as early as

In Kingston Canyon

Stewart Creek, Toiyabe Range

Klondike Mine, Victorine Canyon

Big Creek Canyon

1863, and though ore production did not continue at the level first expected, the canyon has seen several mining revivals. In a little side draw, Victorine Canyon, the old Klondike Mine is being worked again, after the previous owner apparently lost interest. He tunneled in 300 feet and up 120 feet; then, for some reason, he gave up, "six feet short of the vein," according to Arnold Rakow, who was hauling ore out of the mine with an air trammer pulling two ore cars. "After snooping around a bit, we figured this mine might still have some possibilities, so we bought the patented claim. The idea is that we'll give it a try, and if we get some ore, fine. If not, we'll pull out and sell it to somebody else who wants to give it a try."

Three caverns had been blasted out up inside the mountain. The broken rock was being hauled over to the chute with a slusher operated by a feisty old miner, John Jardine. "You damn sure don't care about the weather outside when you're working in a mine all day," he said. "You have to like working by yourself here. You get used to it, though. In fact, after a while you kind of like it. I got a pretty good life here working in the mine; got a little cabin down in the valley, and it's all right."

They'd just started working the mine, after having built a new ore bin, "made by hand with timbers just like the way they used to do it in the old days," said Arnold. "We've got one helluva good prospect here; that's all you can say. You can't

Austin cemetery

Windmill near Tonopah

Raw and finished turquoise

call it a mine yet; it's not proven, but it looks awfully good."

Something else that looks awfully good to many people is turquoise. It was one of the first minerals to be used as a gemstone and was mined even in prehistoric times. Many of the turquoise mines in Nevada today were initially worked centuries ago, by Indians who attributed religious and curative properties to the blue gem. Turquoise was also used as a bartering item among Indian cultures throughout the Southwest.

Though some Indians still consider the stone sacred, it is used primarily as an ornament today, and a popular one at that. Nevada ranks as the largest turquoise producer in the world, supplying jewelers and silversmiths around the country as well as overseas. The more than two dozen mines are located in the high, arid hills and mountains that run down through central Nevada. Each mine produces a distinctive pattern of turquoise, since the nodules and veins of the mineral, which are simply residue from a solution containing copper, phosphorus, aluminum and water, are deposited differently in each place. Many grades of turquoise are found in Nevada mines, and the scarcer top-quality stones here compare well with the most beautiful turquoise in the world.

Though Austin is the center of much turquoise production, it is remembered more for the boom times after silver was discovered in 1862. It's a spirited town still, harking back to the days when people lived with more spunk and gusto

Indian horsemanship

than they do today. Austin's current residents are no less lively and independent than their forebears; they bemoan the fact that they were "born 100 years too late." The traditions of the Sazarac Liars Club continue at the bar in the old International. Named after a popular type of brandy, the Club first flourished during the 1870's with the purpose of providing "mental culture and mutual improvement; we do not lie for greed or gain, nor do we tolerate that class of liars who by word of mouth deceive their fellow-men for wicked or selfish ends...While we permit a range of thought extending far away into the most distant depths of the realm of the impossible, and the improbable, we do not stoop to the lie of deceit; we ask no man to place implicit belief in our lies — but if any man does so believe, he sustains no injury."

A less scrupulous early Austin promoter was able to sell stock in the Reese River Navigation Company to eastern investors. Little did they know that the river was only a few feet wide and hardly deep enough to float a fence post. Today the Reese River Valley is good ranching country and is also being turned into cropland by using groundwater for irrigation. The government has returned part of the upper valley to the Indians, and Henick Smith, a Shoshone, has used the opportunity to build a good ranch. He grazes his cattle in the

Reese River

Henick Smith

surrounding mountains, which also have some of the best stands of piñon pine in the state.

The single-leaf piñon pine, Nevada's state tree, covers hillsides all across the state. The plump, oily seeds of the tree's cones have been a nutritious food source used by the Indians for centuries. The pine "nuts" are very high in protein, and a pound of them contains 3,000 calories. To harvest the nuts, the Indians shook the cones from the trees in the fall and then baked them in a fire; the seeds were then easily removed and roasted.

Although the settlers and miners cut down the piñon forests for firewood and for making charcoal, the hardy pine has grown back. The seeds are still being harvested by the ton, not only by Indians but commercially as well, since the tasty nuts are now considered a gourmet item. Even so, the forests continue to be cut back in order to make more grazing land available to livestock and wildlife.

Another ubiquitous plant in the Nevada landscape is the prickly poppy, which can be found growing in the dry, sandy soils bordering many of the highways. It blossoms forth in April and May with delicately crumpled white petals. Though the spiny stems and leaves make the flowers hard to pick, they are a delight to see, waving in the spring breezes.

Coming across the dusty expanse of Ione Valley, it's hard to imagine that this part of the world was submerged under part of a boundless ocean. But it must have been, as that

Piñon pine cones

Ione Valley

Prickly poppies

seems the only explanation for the presence of over 30 ichthyosaur fossils entombed in the ground among the piñon pines of the Shoshone Mountains. These mammoth marine reptiles, some over 60 feet long and weighing 40 tons, cruised the prehistoric waters 200 million years ago. They were every bit the monsters that surface today only in legends and sea stories. At some point in that ancient time, a school of ichthyosaurs must have been trapped in a shallow inlet when the tide went out. In the geologic upheavals that tore Nevada 30 million years ago, their fossilized remains were lifted with the blocks that formed the Shoshone Mountains. Several million years of erosion have finally revealed them in a most unexpected place. It makes me wonder, as I walk through other hills, how many prehistoric relics and surprises lie hidden, perhaps just inches below the ground, waiting for that last bit of scouring by wind and water before surfacing once again.

A distant cloud of dust way off in the middle of Nevada's broad, sage-covered flats most likely is a band of wild horses on the run. Probably no animal in Nevada stirs up stronger emotions in people than the free-roaming horses. To some they're the living symbol of the spirit of the West; to others they're "just four legs, a tail, and a big head — not good for anything." Over a century ago, the horses numbered in the millions and roamed throughout western America. But they were a nuisance to stockmen, competing with their cattle

and sheep for water and grass. Great numbers of the horses were removed from the range, much as the bison and antelope had been eradicated, and in recent years they declined so drastically (only 16,000 remained in the West by 1969) that they finally received federal protection in 1971. Since then their numbers have swelled again, and over 25,000 wild horses range over Nevada today.

No one I talked with disputed the value of seeing a wild stallion on a ridgetop, its long mane and tail blowing in the wind. The horses do embody a spirited wildness, much like an eagle soaring in the sky. Nor did anyone I talked with deny that the horses need to be managed. The land simply cannot support an ever-increasing number of wild horses, and still provide abundant grazing range for livestock and good habitat for wildlife.

The differences arise in trying to determine just how the horses should be managed. How many wild horses should we have? What should be done with the excess? Basically it is a problem in population control, and one man I talked with said, "It's sort of like trying to decide how to manage people." In a time when our values are constantly being reviewed and changed, it becomes a question of establishing priorities, of deciding just how large a place we're willing to make for things that may have little or no commercial worth.

The wild horse problem is a symptom of a much more basic question in Nevada: who should have stewardship of

Mustangs on the run

Rounding 'em up

Gilding the window

the land? Some 86 percent of Nevada's land is owned and controlled by the federal government — more than in any other state except Alaska. The government's rights to this property date back to the early Indian treaties, though many of them were pure chicanery. There was also a clause in the Nevada State Constitution declaring that "the people inhabiting said Territory do agree and declare, that they forever disclaim all right and title to the unappropriated public lands lying within said Territory, and that the same shall be and remain at the sole and entire disposition of the United States."

All this has led to the irony of the free-willed, independent Nevadans being unable to use their lands freely. Instead they are increasingly hemmed in and restricted by government regulations. On the other hand, many of the ranchers who are so steadfastly proud of their self-sufficiency have in fact been subsidized over the years through their use of public lands. Still, as the government places more restrictions on land use, the rancher has nowhere to go, since there is little private or deeded property available. It seems contradictory to me that the principles used in allocating water resources — those of beneficial and prior use — do not also apply to the allocation of land.

The deterioration of the range during the last few decades raises the question of whether the Bureau of Land Management is the best overseer of Nevada's land. When turned over to private ownership, notably in Diamond Valley, parcels of land have been rejuvenated and become far more productive. But privately-held agricultural land cannot meet all of today's

Joe Clifford and granddaughter

Mule deer

demands on the public domain — the grazing needs of livestock, wildlife, and horses; the recreational activities of an increasingly restive population; mineral exploration and mining; and the need to protect wilderness areas and resources for future generations. The problem is one of how best to allocate what we now realize are limited resources in the face of growing and diverging requirements. The dilemma carries an extra burden of responsibility today: we are obliged to learn from past mistakes. Nevada is unique in that wide expanses of the state have escaped much of the environmental degradation occurring elsewhere in the country. But that may be deceiving. The raw, rugged vastness of this mountain and desert country, its air and its water, are no less fragile than in other, more temperate areas.

Joe and Roy Clifford live with their families out in the wide-open country of central Nevada. Their roots in this land date back to the 1860's, when their father homesteaded next to a spring in the middle of Stone Cabin Valley. It's a harsh, demanding land, and few people understand it better than the Cliffords. They are men with a sense of purpose, a firm grasp on what life is all about, which seems to be less evident among people in more crowded places. Out here, if something needs to be done, the best way to get it done is to *do it*, and any authority that threatens to restrict a man's ability to act on necessity is naturally regarded with deep suspicion. Out here, the only authority is survival.

Diamond Mountains

Manhattan church

If the Cliffords are steadfastly independent, ruggedly self-reliant, they are also decent, honestly warm people, who gave a complete stranger nosing around taking pictures more than the benefit of the doubt. I was surprised when Roy invited me in for a cup of coffee and stopped watching a football game on television to talk for an hour. Until about 20 years ago, Stone Cabin Valley was part of the last uncontrolled open range in the country. The Clifford family had been making a good living on their ranch for nearly a hundred years. Then the government started "managing" the land, and soon, according to Roy, "there were so many government agencies swarming around, making life difficult, acting like they owned everything under the sun — a lot of this is patented land; we own it. Every now and then I get so fed up with those damn bureaucrats I kick 'em off." Clifford can't see why the government wants to spend so much of the taxpayer's money rounding up wild horses only to give them away, when the ranchers would do it themselves. Obviously there have been abuses; but other practices, such as hunting and even land development, aren't indiscriminately outlawed when a few people are caught stepping out of line.

It's becoming more and more difficult for the Cliffords to hang onto their way of life. Because of overgrazing by both livestock and wild horses, the government is increasing grazing fees and restricting the use of the range in order to improve it. Other costs are going up, and the cattlemen are being

Garfield Flat

Shield-leaf peppergrass

squeezed by the beef buyers and middlemen. In effect, the rancher is paying more and getting less, and is forced to put even more pressure on the land to make a living.

The authentic spirit of the frontier, which has always been a curious mix of cantankerousness, neighborliness, stubbornness, selfishness, humor and humanitarianism, and which is still alive in families like the Cliffords, may be in jeopardy even in Nevada. Those who embody it clearly intend to fight to live as they have chosen, just as the wild stallion fights to evade capture. Both represent a disappearing distinction of our national heritage. I hope they both can be preserved. I can't believe the world has gotten so small that there's no longer room for people like the Cliffords, and for the wild horse as well.

Above all this earth-bound drama loom the mountains, rising indomitably out of the desert openness of Nevada. Their sobering permanency is a powerful reminder that some things will always transcend and endure the manipulations and quarrelings of mankind. Their timeless grandeur moves us, in the words of Walter Van Tilberg Clark, Nevada's leading novelist, to "believe in the effects of a bigger time, where the lives of single men wink in and out like the glitterings on windy water."

Nevada Textures

Always a contrast

From 500 miles up, and through the lens of a satellite-mounted infrared camera, Nevada presents an unusually colorful mosaic. Areas of vigorously growing, healthy vegetation — whether irrigated croplands, watered lawns, or forested regions — show up in shades of red. Clear lakes are a very dark blue, while waters clouded with sediment are turquoise in color. The alkali flats and desert lands which lack any appreciable vegetation are white, as are the clouds and any snow in the mountains. The green-blue and grey-blue shades represent areas with little moisture and sparse growth: sage and grasslands, fallow fields, and areas with desert plants like cactus, Joshua, and yucca.

Lake Tahoe stands out in the upper left photograph, with the Truckee River winding down to Reno. Washoe Lake and the Carson Valley are also distinct; the Carson River meanders east into Lahontan Reservoir. To the right, the north-south horseshoe-shaped course of the Walker River can be followed; Mason Valley and the agricultural lands around Fallon are sharply defined. Clouds hover over Mount Grant and Cory Peak, south of Walker Lake. On the lower left are Lake Mead and the Colorado River, and nearby Las Vegas; to the west rise the Sandstone Bluffs, but not as massively as the Ruby Mountains in the lower right photograph. Most of the water flows west out of the Rubys and into Huntington Valley, and then into the Humboldt River.

To get back down to earth and out into the land, with senses wide open, is to be awed by the richness and variety, the sheer power and simple beauty, that is evident across the state. The photographs on the following pages are an invitation to take a closer look at Nevada, at the textures that stand apart in discernable contrast, or blend together to reveal another facet of nature's supreme design.

Because of the grand scale of that design in Nevada, there is a tendency to overlook the details — a play of light and shadow, a delicate symmetry, a newly perceived pattern. "In other places, beauty can be found anywhere; it's too commonplace. But in Nevada," according to one long-time resident, "you have to look for it. Usually not very far, though, because you learn to appreciate what you can see."

I would go just a bit further, and say that first you learn to see in a new way. There is challenge in this, of course, but many people find that rewarding. Certainly Nevadans do; challenge is a way of life to them, and their proud independence, their self-confidence and open friendliness are some of the dividends they enjoy, living as they do, close to the rugged, wide-open land.

"One of the best-paying professions is getting ahold of pieces of country in your mind, learning their smell and their moods, sorting out the pieces of a view, deciding what grows there and there and why, how many steps that hill will take, where this creek winds and where it meets the other one below, what elevation timberline is now…This is the best kind of ownership, and the most permanent" (from *On The Loose*). Many such pieces of country make up a special place called Nevada — worth discovering again and again!

Curlicues of a yucca

Aspen bark

Natural montage

Elegant design

Desert birdcage

Big Smokey Valley

Spare wheels

Sunbleached siding

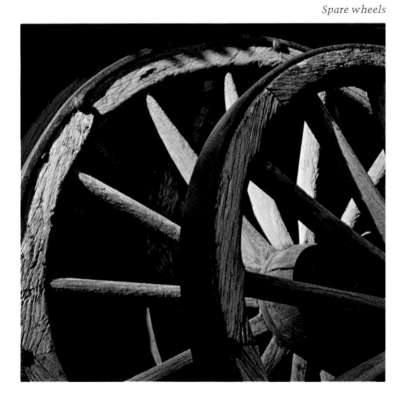

Wooden gravemarker

Doorlatch

Rock wall patterns

Desert collage

Photography Credits

About the Photography

A great many of the photographs in this book reflect the sensitivity, perception and talents of Jack Williams. He traveled with us on most of our field trips through Nevada, tirelessly recording his impressions on film from daybreak to sunset. Nearly 20 percent of the color photographs in the book are Jack's; they speak for themselves.

All told, we screened more than 15,000 photographs for the book, taken by both amateurs and professionals. The selection process was arduous, to say the least. Color balance between photographs, our ability to crop them to fit the book's design, and story line were the deciding criteria. A good majority of the photographs were 35 mm transparencies. A few 2¼ x 2¼ and several 4 x 5 transparencies were also used.

We are grateful to all the photographers who patiently let us keep their material through the several months required to collect and screen photographs and then lay out the pages of the book. We believe their pictures have given the book an appealing variety that could be achieved no other way.

Contributing Photographers

Ashman, David	McLane, Alvin
Bauer, Erwin A.	Mellender, Keith
Beatty, David	Mitchell, Roger
Beatty, Robert O.	Mitrani, Frank
Bundy, Gus	Morris, Toby
Campbell, Gordon S.	Muench, Bonnie
Cooper, Ed	Muench, David
Davis, Jim	Mullins, Bill
Dufurrena, Linda	Naskali, Richard J.
Duvall, Owen	Ottenheimer, Miles
Erickson, Duane	Page, Jerry L.
Flannery, John S.	Perry, Danny
Flock, Allan	Peterson, Ernst
Fuller, William H.	Reinheller, Jim
Germino, Bill	Rowan, Dick
Goodman, Robert J.	Ryczkowski, John J.
Hadley, Caroline J.	Scovill, Ed
Heller, Alan M.	Segerblom, Cliff
Herlan, Peter J.	Sigler, Kim
Houghton, John	Vanderford, James D.
Lawrence, James A.	Webber, David
Lockard, Dale	Williams, Jack
Marston, Art	Yoakum, Jim

Other Photography Sources

The Bancroft Library
Chester Barton Collection
Ron Bommarito Collection
Mrs. Jack Burns Collection
Earth Resources Observation Systems Data Center
Harrah's Hotels & Casinos
Frances Humphrey Collection
National Archives and Records Service
Nevada Department of Fish & Game
Nevada Historical Society
Nevada Outdoor Recreation Association
Nevada State Museum
Stanley W. Paher Collection
Goldie Howard Redicon Collection
Smithsonian Institution, Anthropological Archives
The Society of California Pioneers
Studios Kaminski
Mark Twain Memorial, Hartford, Conn.
Special Collections Department, University of Nevada Reno Library
Dilla Woodruff Collection

Acknowledgments

A book like this doesn't get put together without the help of many, many people. It's impossible to name them all, but a few deserve special mention.

First of all, Alvin McLane, whose research and travels in the state have made him a fount of information on Nevada, gave tirelessly of his time and energy, as well as contributing many photographs. Another major source of photographs and information was Jim Yoakum, wildlife biologist with the BLM. Caroline Hadley, managing editor of *Nevada Magazine*, not only helped us to locate photographers and verified some of our ideas, but was also a continual source of encouragement. Eslie Cann and Jim Higgins, at the Nevada State Historical Society, and Pam Crowell, at the Nevada State Museum, were always able to find time to help us track down historical facts and photographs. Both Stan Paher and Walt Mulcahy permitted us to look at their collections of early-day photographs and helped with identification.

As we traveled through the state we met many people like Ruth and Tony Tipton, who live on a ranch near Winnemucca and freely shared much of their time and many of their insights on living in Nevada. Tony even took time to fly us over northern Nevada one day, showing us what the country looks like from the air.

Roy Clifford, a second-generation Nevada rancher, Velma Johnston, of the Wild Horse Organized Assistance foundation, and Charles Watson of the Nevada Outdoor Recreation Association, all shared with us their perceptions on the volatile issues of wild horses and land use in Nevada.

At the Nevada Department of Fish and Game, Bob Sumner, Dale Lockard, Glen Christensen and Charley Crunden were very willing to help us out with information or photographs of wildlife in the state. Doc Kaminski and Ken Kruger at Studios Kaminski, Ltd., were helpful in making available their photograph files, and in reprinting many of the early-day photographs used in the book.

Jim Deacon, head of the Biology Department at the University of Nevada, Las Vegas, explained the controversy over pupfish; and Dick Naskali, an assistant professor of botany at the University of Idaho, provided us with information on many aspects of botany and geology in Nevada.

We thank all of these people, and all the others who gave of their time and energy to make this book possible — particularly Dave Quinn and Art Smith at the First National Bank of Nevada, who gave us unwavering support throughout the project.

Bibliography

Armstrong, Margaret. *Field Book of Western Wild Flowers.* New York: G. P. Putnam's Sons, 1915.

Bailey, Paul. *Ghost Dance Messiah.* Los Angeles: Westernlore Press, 1970.

Bennett, Edna Mae. *Turquoise and the Indian.* Denver: Sage Books, 1966.

Carlson, Helen S. *Nevada Place Names: A Geographical Dictionary.* Reno: University of Nevada Press, 1974.

Clark, Walter Van Tilburg. *City of Trembling Leaves.* New York: Random House, 1945.

Dangberg, Grace. *Carson Valley: Historical Sketches of Nevada's First Settlement.* Reno: The Carson Valley Historical Society, 1973.

Douglass, William A. "The Basques of the American West: Preliminary Historical Perspectives." *Nevada Historical Society Quarterly* 13 (1970):13-25.

Edwards, Elbert B. "Early Mormon Settlements in Southern Nevada." *Nevada Historical Society Quarterly* 8 (1965):25-44.

Elliott, Russell R. *History of Nevada.* Lincoln: University of Nebraska, 1973.

Forbes, Jack D. *Nevada Indians Speak.* Reno: University of Nevada Press, 1967.

Glass, Mary Ellen. "The First Nationally Sponsored Arid Land Reclamation Project: The Newlands Act in Churchill County, Nevada." *Nevada Historical Society Quarterly* 14 (1971):2-12.

History of Nevada, 1881. Reproduction. Berkeley: Howell-North, 1958.

Jackson, Donald Dale. *Sagebrush Country: The American Wilderness.* New York: Time-Life Books, 1975.

King, Richard. *Graveyard of the Giants: The Story of Berlin-Ichthyosaur State Park and Environs.* Reprinted from *Nevada Outdoors And Wildlife Review,* Summer Edition, Vol. 6, No. 2, 1972. Sponsored by Nevada State Park Natural History Association.

Lavender, David. *The American Heritage History of The Great West.* New York: American Heritage Publishing Company, Inc., 1965.

Laxalt, Robert. *The Other Nevada.* Reprinted from the June 1974 *National Geographic.* Washington: National Geographic Society, 1974.

Lewis, Oscar. *The Town That Died Laughing.* Boston: Little, Brown and Company, 1955.

Lillard, Richard G. *Desert Challenge: An Interpretation of Nevada.* Lincoln: University of Nebraska Press, 1942.

Lord, Eliot. *Comstock Mining and Miners.* 1883. Reprint. Berkeley: Howell-North, 1959.

McLane, Alvin. "Nevada Caves." *Nevada Highway News* 13, October 1972: 3-8.

Mills, Lester W. *A Sagebrush Saga.* Springville, Utah: Art City Publishing Company, 1956.

Murbarger, Nell. *Sovereigns Of The Sage.* Palm Desert, Calif.: Desert Magazine Press, 1958.

Nevada Wildlife. Centennial Issue, Vol. 5, No.'s 4, 5, 6, 7. Nevada Fish & Game Commission, 1965.

Paher, Stanley W. *Las Vegas: As it began — as it grew.* Las Vegas: Nevada Publications, 1971.

Paher, Stanley W. *Nevada Ghost Towns & Mining Camps.* Berkeley: Howell-North Books, 1970.

Patterson, Edna B.; Ulph, Louise A.; and Goodwin, Victor. *Nevada's Northwest Frontier.* Sparks, Nev.: Western Printing & Publishing Company, 1969.

Political History of Nevada 1973. Sixth Edition. Issued by William D. Swackhamer, Secretary of State. Carson City: State of Nevada, 1974.

Rideing, William H. "The Wheeler Survey In Nevada." *Harper's New Monthly* LV-325-5: 65-76.

Russell, Terry and Renny. *On The Loose.* San Francisco: Sierra Club, 1967.

Scott, Edward B. *The Saga of Lake Tahoe.* Lake Tahoe, Nev.: Sierra-Tahoe Publishing Company, 1957.

Strong, Emory. *Stone Age In The Great Basin.* Portland, Ore.: Binfords & Mort, 1969.

U.S. Geological Survey and Nevada Bureau of Mines. *Mineral And Water Resources Of Nevada.* Bulletin 65. Reno: Mackay School of Mines, University of Nevada, 1964.

Watkins, T. H. and Watson, Charles S., Jr. *The Land No One Knows: America and the Public Domain.* San Francisco: Sierra Club Books, 1975.

Wheeler, Sessions S. *The Desert Lake: The Story of Nevada's Pyramid Lake.* Caldwell, Idaho: The Caxton Printers, Ltd., 1974.

Wheeler, Sessions S. *The Nevada Desert.* Caldwell, Idaho: The Caxton Printers, Ltd., 1972.

Woon, Basil. *The Why, How and Where of Gambling in Nevada.* Reno: Bonanza Publishing Company, 1953.

Writers' Project, Nevada Historical Society. *Nevada: A Guide To The Silver State.* American Guide Series. Portland, Ore.: Binfords & Mort, 1940.

*Text photocomposed in 10 on 12 Trump Medieval,
with Trump bold heads and Dominante display.*

*Color separations and printing by Sweeney, Krist & Dimm,
Portland, Oregon. Lithography by four-color sheetfed
offset on 100 lb. Vintage Velvet text.*

*Binding by Lincoln & Allen, Portland, Oregon,
in Columbia Mills Bolton Natural,
hot foil stamped in silver and clear foil
with endsheets of Multicolor Textured;
one hundred presentation copies bound in antique finish cowhide
and slipcased in Columbia Mills Bolton Natural.*

*Design and graphic production by Walter Justus
of R. O. Beatty & Associates, Boise, Idaho.*

A Beatty Book